U.S. Fish & Wildlife Service

Revised Comprehensive Conservation Plan

Alaska Peninsula and Becharof National Wildlife Refuges

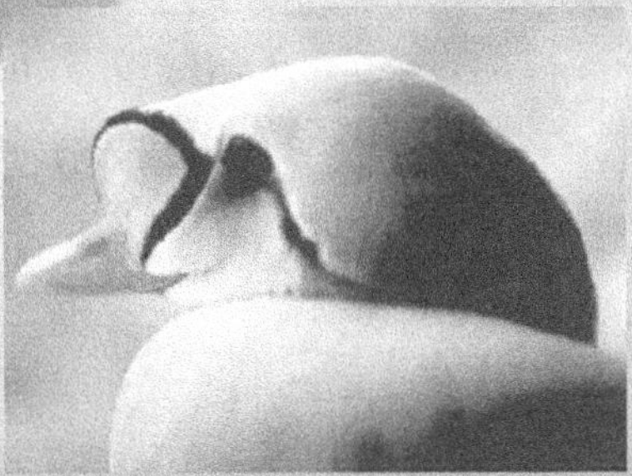

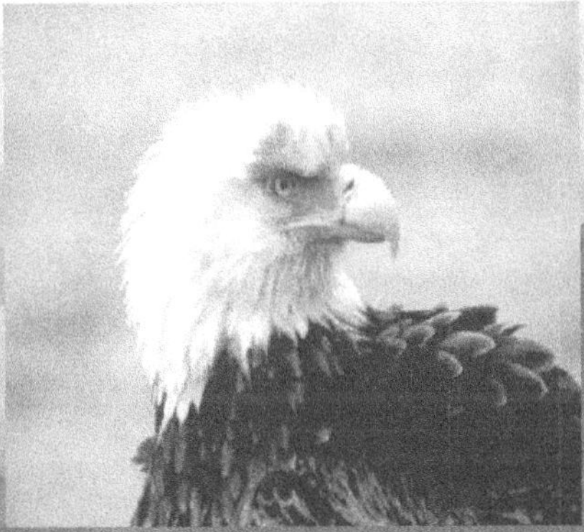

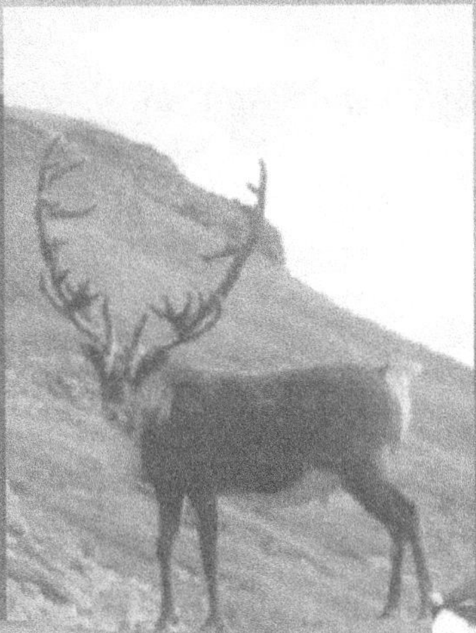

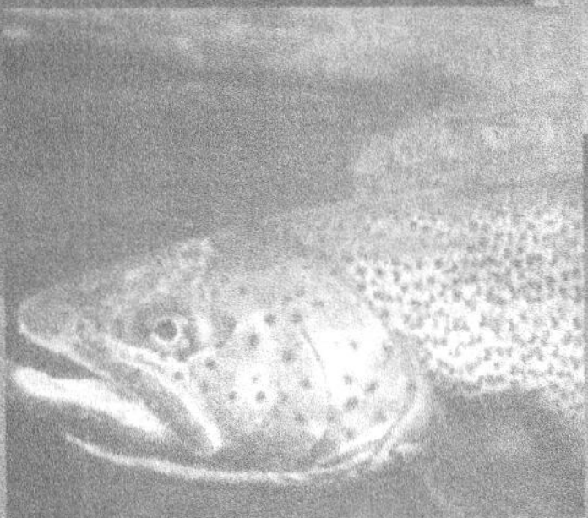

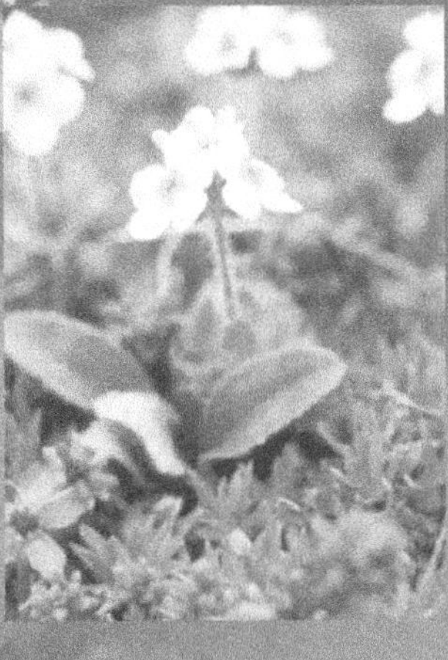

U.S. Fish and Wildlife Service Mission Statement

The mission of the U.S. Fish and Wildlife Service is working with others to conserve, protect, and enhance fish, wildlife, plants, and their habitats for the continuing benefit of the American people.

Refuge Mission Statement

The mission of the National Wildlife Refuge System is to administer a national network of lands and waters for the conservation, management, and, where appropriate, restoration of the fish, wildlife, and plant resources and their habitats within the United States for the benefit of present and future generations of Americans.

—National Wildlife Refuge System Improvement Act of 1997

The comprehensive conservation plan details program planning levels that are substantially greater than current budget allocations and, as such, is for strategic planning and program prioritization purposes only. This plan does not constitute a commitment for staffing increases or funding for future refuge-specific land acquisitions, construction projects, or operational and maintenance increases.

Revised Comprehensive Conservation Plan

Alaska Peninsula
And
Becharof
National Wildlife Refuges

May 2006

Prepared by:
U.S. Fish and Wildlife Service
Region 7
Anchorage, Alaska

Alaska Peninsula and Becharof
National Wildlife Refuges
P.O. Box 277
King Salmon, AK 99613

U.S. Fish and Wildlife Service
Region 7
1011 East Tudor Rd.
Anchorage, AK 99503

Dear Reader,

This Revised Comprehensive Conservation Plan (Conservation Plan) presents management direction for the Alaska Peninsula and Becharof National Wildlife Refuges. It represents the preferred alternative, 3a, in the *"Revised Comprehensive Conservation Plan and Environmental Impact Statement: Alaska Peninsula and Becharof National Wildlife Refuges"* of October 2005. That Plan combined and updated the 1985 and 1987 Plans and incorporated a revision of the 1994 Public Use Management Plan.

This Conservation Plan covers the Becharof National Wildlife Refuge, the Ugashik and Chignik units of the Alaska Peninsula National Wildlife Refuge, and the Seal Cape area of Alaska Maritime National Wildlife Refuge. These units, all managed by the U.S. Fish & Wildlife Service office in King Salmon, will be referred to as the Alaska Peninsula and Becharof Refuges or simply as "the Refuges."

The *"Revised Comprehensive Conservation Plan and Environmental Impact Statement: Alaska Peninsula and Becharof National Wildlife Refuges"* of October 2005 contains background information, alternatives, and the environmental effects of implementing the plan. That information is not included in this document.

Comments or requests for further information may be addressed to:

Refuge Manager	or	Chief
Alaska Peninsula and Becharof		Division of Conservation
National Wildlife Refuges		Planning and Policy
P.O. Box 277		U.S. Fish and Wildlife Service
King Salmon, AK 99613		1011 East Tudor Rd.
		Anchorage, AK 99503

Table of Contents

Acronyms

ADF&G	Alaska Department of Fish & Game
ANCSA	Alaska Native Claims Settlement Act
ANHA	Alaska Natural History Association
ANILCA	Alaska National Interest Lands Conservation Act
DLP	defense of life or property
DNR	Alaska Department of Natural Resources
EIS	environmental impact statement
GIS	geographic information systems
GMU	game management unit
I&M	inventory and monitoring
IACUC	Institutional Animal Care and Use Committee
KSVC	King Salmon Visitor Center
LPP	land protection plan
MAPS	Monitoring Avian Productivity and Survivorship
NEPA	National Environmental Policy Act
ORV	off-road vehicle
PUMP	public-use management plan
RAWS	Remote Area Weather Stations
RONS	Refuge Operational Needs System
Service	U.S. Fish & Wildlife Service
System	National Wildlife Refuge System
USGS	U.S. Geological Survey

1. Introduction

The Refuges comprise approximately 4.2 million acres on the Alaska Peninsula (Figure 1). The northern boundary of the Becharof Refuge lies approximately 10 miles south of King Salmon. The refuge extends south past Becharof Lake, where it meets the northern boundary of the Ugashik Unit of the Alaska Peninsula Refuge. The Alaska Peninsula Refuge stretches for nearly 340 miles along the peninsula and is divided into four management units. The Ugashik and Chignik units are separated by the Aniakchak National Monument and Preserve. The Seal Cape area is part of the Alaska Maritime Refuge. The most southern portions of the Alaska Peninsula National Wildlife Refuge—the Pavlof and North Creek units—are managed by the Izembek National Wildlife Refuge; and they are not covered by this plan.

Figure 1: Refuge Locations

This Comprehensive Conservation Plan contains management direction from the 2005 *"Revised Comprehensive Conservation Plan and Environmental Impact Statement: Alaska Peninsula and Becharof National Wildlife Refuges"*. It replaces the previous management direction for these refuges which was described in the Comprehensive Conservation Plans adopted in 1985 for the Becharof Refuge (USFWS 1985) and in 1987 for the Alaska Peninsula Refuge (USFWS 1987). This plan also replaces the 1994 Public Use Management Plan for the Refuges.

The *"Revised Comprehensive Conservation Plan and Environmental Impact Statement: Alaska Peninsula and Becharof National Wildlife Refuges"* (October 2005) contains background information and the full

National Environmental Policy Act (NEPA) analysis which was conducted during its development.

1.1 Refuge Establishment

In 1978, President Jimmy Carter established the 1,157,000-acre Becharof National Wildlife Monument with Presidential Proclamation 4613. The monument was established to protect the area, notably the unique brown bear denning islands in the Island Arm of Becharof Lake. (Figure 2: Becharof National Wildlife Refuge

In 1980, Section 302 of ANILCA established the Alaska Peninsula National Wildlife Refuge and changed the Becharof National Wildlife Monument into a national wildlife refuge. Section 303(1) of ANILCA created the Alaska Maritime National Wildlife Refuge by redesignating 11 pre-existing refuges as units of the new refuge and adding other public lands on island, islets, rocks, reefs, spires, and designated capes and headlands in the coastal areas and adjacent seas of Alaska.

In 1983, the Service decided to manage the Ugashik and Chignik units (figures 3 pg 125 and 4 pg 127) of the Alaska Peninsula Refuge, the 9,900-acre Seal Cape area of the Alaska Maritime Refuge, and the Becharof Refuge as a "complex" because they shared resources and resource issues. Distance and weather create barriers to managing the Pavlof and North Creek units of the Alaska Peninsula Refuge from the King Salmon office; so management of these units was shifted to the Izembek Refuge headquartered in Cold Bay.

1.2 Refuge Purposes

The primary purposes of the Alaska Peninsula and Becharof Refuges are described in Section 302(1)B) and Section 302(2)(B) of ANILCA. Purposes for the Alaska Maritime National Wildlife Refuge are described in Section 303(1)(B).

These purposes include the following (unless otherwise noted, the purposes apply to all units of the Refuges):

- *[Alaska Maritime]* to conserve fish and wildlife populations and habitats in their natural diversity, including marine mammals, marine birds, and other migratory birds, the marine resources upon which they rely, bears, caribou, and other mammals

- *[Alaska Peninsula]* to conserve fish and wildlife populations and habitats in their natural diversity, including brown bears, the Alaska Peninsula caribou herd, moose, sea otters and other marine mammals, shorebirds and other migratory birds, raptors including bald eagles and peregrine falcons, and salmonids and other fish

- *[Becharof]* to conserve fish and wildlife populations and habitats in their natural diversity, including brown bears, salmon, migratory birds, the Alaska Peninsula caribou herd, and marine mammals and birds

- to fulfill the international treaty obligations of the United States with respect to fish and wildlife and their habitats

- to provide, in a manner consistent with the purposes set forth in preceding paragraphs, the opportunity for continued subsistence uses by local residents

- *[Alaska Maritime]* to provide, in a manner consistent with preceding paragraphs, a program of national and international scientific research on marine resources

- to ensure to the maximum extent practicable and in a manner consistent with the purposes set forth in preceding text, water quality and necessary water quantity within the refuge

- *[Becharof Wilderness Area]* to secure an enduring resource of wilderness, to protect and preserve the wilderness character of areas within the National Wilderness Resource Preservation System, and to administer this wilderness for the use and enjoyment of the American people in a way that will leave it unimpaired for future use and enjoyment as wilderness.

2. Refuge Management

Goals and objectives focus management of the Refuges. These, when combined with refuge management direction, provide management direction for the Refuges. The primary sources of this management direction are the various laws governing the National Wildlife Refuge System and the regulations, policies, and other guidance—both national and regional—developed to implement these laws.

2.1 Vision Statement

The Alaska Peninsula and Becharof Refuges will remain as they are today with healthy, natural populations of fish and wildlife living in primarily unaltered habitats. The Refuges will continue to provide local residents opportunities for subsistence use. The Refuges will be open to all people to engage in a variety of wildlife-dependent activities and to enjoy the spectacular setting and resources. Refuge management and outreach will be a model of effective collaboration among diverse public interests and public and private landowners and managers.

2.2 Refuge Goals and Objectives

The refuge vision statement and purposes provide the framework for developing goals and objectives for managing the Refuges.

The objectives listed beneath each goal are often applicable to more than one goal. In order to avoid unnecessary duplication, we have listed each objective only once, under the goal that represents the clearest connection. The ordering of the objectives is not intended to imply prioritization; in fact, the many objectives listed beneath Goal 2 have been clustered into rough categories of wildlife, habitat, and fish. Following each objective, we list those other goals the objectives are also designed to address.

Many of the objectives that are important for managing subsistence activities and public use of the Refuges require monitoring or improving our knowledge of the natural resources linked to the subsistence or public-use activities. For this reason, most of the objectives for subsistence or public use are listed beneath Goal 1 or Goal 2, the two of which are focused on improving our knowledge of the Refuges' biological resources and on conserving habitat for those resources.

Goal 1: *Ensure quantity and optimal quality of naturally functioning habitats available on the Refuges for fish and wildlife populations in perpetuity, especially for salmonids, migratory birds, the Northern Alaska Peninsula caribou herd, moose, and brown bear*

The Refuge vision statement and purposes emphasize conserving populations and habitats in their natural diversity. Although fish and wildlife populations may fluctuate for a variety of reasons, if the habitats on which they depend are functioning naturally and available in their natural abundance and diversity, the opportunity exists for populations to thrive. As with many of the other refuges in Alaska, the size, remoteness, weather, and complexity of the Alaska Peninsula and Becharof Refuges make it challenging to collect data on species and habitats. Fulfilling this goal requires information about fish, wildlife, and plant populations and their relationship to the habitat. Almost all of the objectives stated under Goal 2 and Goal 4 are objectives that would also provide necessary information for achieving Goal 1.

1. Delineate marbled godwit nesting habitat and range in the Ugashik and Cinder drainages and vicinity by 2008 (also Goal 2).
2. Cooperate with the State of Alaska in developing an interagency study of traditional subsistence access prior to the Alaska National Interest Lands Conservation Act (ANILCA) and develop and implement methodology to formally monitor existing off-road vehicle impacts on refuge lands by 2010. Monitoring off-road impacts would be conducted to document damage to vegetative cover and soils in areas of significant use, including Big Creek, King Salmon River (near Egegik), Becharof Lake outlet, Yantarni Bay airstrip, and Port Heiden (also Goals 2, 3, and 7).

3. Monitor development of inholdings and uses of adjacent parcels to identify activities that could adversely affect refuge users and resources. Work with Service's Regional Office realty specialists to identify opportunities to acquire lands or interests in lands from willing sellers to further the goals of the refuge and the mission of the National Wildlife Refuge System. Additional assistance may be provided by working with other federal agencies, the state, Native corporations, and nongovernmental organizations.

Goal 2: *Improve knowledge of fish and wildlife populations and their habitats in order to conserve species in their natural diversity, especially those that are identified in the refuge purposes, that have restricted populations, or that have been identified as species or populations of ecological interest*

The Refuges' objectives for wildlife under Goal 2 are directed toward monitoring a diverse group of species, including moose, caribou, wolves, bears, waterfowl, bald eagles, seabirds, shorebirds, and songbirds. This monitoring will provide valuable information for the ongoing management of wildlife populations on the Refuges as well as for responding to catastrophic events. These inventory and monitoring objectives will be incorporated in the wildlife inventory plan and may be revised when the Refuges staff completes a formal review of the biological program. Successful completion of many objectives will require close cooperation or consultation with the Alaska Department of Fish & Game (ADF&G), other agencies, the academic community, residents with local knowledge, and/or others.

4. Complete the Refuges' wildlife inventory plan—which includes goals and objectives, priorities, and methods for wildlife monitoring and inventory—by October 2007 (also Goal 1).
5. Estimate moose density in the Refuges and vicinity, using professionally accepted methods, by 2008 (also Goals 1 and 3).
6. Contribute to international efforts to establish trends in migratory bird populations by inventorying and monitoring landbird populations (as scheduled in the wildlife inventory plan) for measures of abundance, reproduction, and habitat using methods such as Monitoring Avian Productivity and Survivorship (MAPS) program, point counts, Christmas bird counts, and fall migration monitoring (also Goal 1).
7. Evaluate the Mother Goose Lake MAPS sites, in coordination with Boreal Partners in Flight and the Institute for Bird Populations, to determine if MAPS monitoring should be continued periodically, reinitiated in the future, or initiated at a new location. Implement schedule as recommended (also Goal 1).
8. Cooperate with other land managers to inventory and monitor shorebirds in the Bristol Bay lowlands.
9. Cooperate with other land managers to monitor population trends of productivity of swans in the Bristol Bay lowlands.
10. Continue monitoring (as scheduled in the wildlife inventory plan) waterfowl staging in upper Bristol Bay drainages during spring to document the range and annual variation of species composition, abundance, and phenology (timing) for use as a baseline for long-term impacts from local development and for

the transition into spring waterfowl hunting (also Goal 3).

11. Conduct year-round monitoring of waterfowl harvested by local villagers (also Goal 3).

12. Continue cooperation with ADF&G on inventory, monitoring, and research studies to maximize information available for the management of species such as moose, caribou, brown bear, and others (also Goals 1 and 3).

13. In cooperation with ADF&G, by 2010, develop methodology and begin gathering information on trapping effort, harvest, and areas within the Refuges (also Goals 3 and 6).

14. Survey caribou (as scheduled in the wildlife inventory plan) in Pacific drainages of the Chignik Unit to determine post-calving count and calf composition (also Goal 3).

15. Monitor Pacific coast murre colonies of Becharof Refuge for peak colony count and productivity in three of every 10 years in order to document recovery from the Exxon Valdez oil spill (also Goal 1).

16. Monitor bald eagle populations and productivity along the Pacific coast of the Refuges every five years and initiate inventory of eagles in Bristol Bay drainages and of other raptors throughout the Refuges by 2008.

17. Develop methodology and monitor wolf numbers and predation on caribou and moose in the Refuges and vicinity by 2008 (also Goal 3).

18. Monitor seabird colony numbers along the Pacific coast of the Refuges, in cooperation with the Alaska Maritime Refuge, every 10 years (also Goal 1).

19. Continue inventory and monitoring of rodent and insectivore distributions and trends on the Refuges.

Knowledge of wildlife habitat characteristics such as distribution, quality, function, and availability is an important first step in understanding changes in wildlife populations. The following objectives were established to develop the necessary information and tools for a basic understanding of wildlife habitat on the Refuges.

20. Complete development, by 2008, of a refuge-based geographic information system (GIS); hardware, software, and data layers) that provides managers and biologists with a basic capability for mapping available data (also Goal 1).

21. Assist the Service's Alaska regional botanist in completing the vegetation community classification for the Refuges (also Goal 1).

22. Determine range condition for the Northern Alaska Peninsula caribou herd by 2010 (also Goal 1).

23. Complete a habitat inventory plan that includes goals, objectives, priorities, and methods for habitat inventory and monitoring by December 2007 (also Goal 1).

24. Develop a map of major vegetation types and mosaics—incorporating soils, surficial geology, and water—for the Refuges and vicinity by 2010 (also Goal 1)

25. Develop habitat models and maps for caribou and moose on the Refuges and vicinity by 2012 (also Goal 1).

26. Develop habitat models and maps for additional species (following the completion of habitat maps for caribou and moose) using priorities established in the wildlife and habitat inventory plans at a rate of one habitat map per year (also Goals

1 and 3).

27. Complete reconnaissance of invasive plant and animal species near communities, ports, and other access points by 2010 (also Goal 1).

28. Determine, by 2006, whether caribou summering in Pacific drainages of the Ugashik Unit constitute a distinct subpopulation of the Northern Alaska Peninsula caribou herd (also Goals 1 and 3).

29. In cooperation with ADF&G and the National Park Service, conduct wildlife inventories, monitoring, and research on species—including caribou, moose, and brown bear—to increase information available for management (also Goal 3).

30. Continue working cooperatively with partners to complete ongoing studies and projects and initiate other high-priority projects identified during the Becharof Ecosystem Partnership Workshop (March 1997). Some of the highest-priority projects concern learning more about the population dynamics of the Northern Alaska Peninsula caribou herd; expanding resident and anadromous fisheries baseline data; completing vegetative cover and habitat mapping; monitoring water quality; and quantifying public uses (also Goals 1, 3, 6, and 7).

31. Work with partners to contribute to understanding of climatic changes and their effects on refuge resources.

32. Continue to operate Remote Area Weather Stations (RAWS) at Mother Goose Lake and Yantarni for collection of weather information.

The following objectives are designed to increase understanding of, and the ability to manage, important fish populations on the Refuges. The objectives address species and drainages that are important not only for subsistence, commercial, and recreation uses, but also for their contribution to the ecological integrity of the Refuges.

33. Evaluate Arctic grayling, lake trout, and Dolly Varden population structure and abundance in the Ugashik and Egegik drainages by 2006.

34. Evaluate coho salmon population structure and abundance in the Pacific coast and Bering Sea drainages by 2010 (also Goal 3).

35. Evaluate Chinook salmon population structure and abundance in the Bering Sea drainages by 2010 (also Goal 3).

36. Reevaluate rainbow trout population structure and abundance in the King Salmon River by 2008 (also Goal 3).

37. Conduct creel surveys of the winter fishery in the lower King Salmon River, Egegik drainage, by 2015 (also Goal 3).

38. Conduct creel surveys of the summer open-water fishery at the Ugashik Lakes by 2006 (also Goals 6 and 7).

39. Continue implementation of the Fisheries Management Plan of 1994 and update the plan by 2008 (also Goals 1 and 3).

Goal 3: *Provide opportunities for local residents to continue their subsistence use of the Refuges, consistent with the subsistence priority and other refuge purposes*

The opportunity for continued subsistence use by local residents is one of the purposes for which the Refuges were established by ANILCA. Objectives for this goal are directed at working with local residents and others to understand subsistence uses and potential conflicts and to monitor subsistence resources for better management. Most of the objectives related to subsistence resources are listed under Goal 2.

40. Continue the Refuge Information Technician program to enhance information exchange with local communities on subsistence issues (also Goal 8).

41. Continue monitoring hunter activity in areas of potential conflict between local and outside hunters and investigate allegations of interference (also Goal 7).

42. Continue to participate in the fish and game regulation process through local fish and game advisory committees, the Alaska Boards of Fisheries and Game, the Subsistence Regional Advisory Council, the Alaska Migratory Bird Co-management Council, and the Federal Subsistence Board to facilitate information exchange and rule-making (also Goal 6).

43. Cooperate with the Federal Subsistence Board in making customary and traditional use determinations for refuge-area communities, including for finfish and beaver.

44. Expand law-enforcement activities to increase education and outreach, field patrols, and investigation of cases associated with the implementation of spring waterfowl hunting regulations (also Goal 8).

Goal 4: *Improve baseline understanding of water resources on the Refuges to acquire and maintain the water quality and quantity necessary to conserve fish and wildlife populations and habitats in their natural diversity.*

Objectives for water quality and quantity are directed at supporting Goals 1 and 4 and completing baseline studies and acquiring the necessary rights to protect water quality and quantity, as directed by the purposes of the Refuges, as established in ANILCA.

45. Complete or update an inventory and assessment of refuge water resources—including quantity, quality, use, and protection status—by 2008. (also Goal 1).

46. Based on the inventory and assessment (objective 45), complete, by 2010, a study plan to investigate the water resources of the Refuges to maintain the quality and quantity to protect the fish, wildlife, and habitats of the refuges in their natural diversity.

47. Analyze and determine water-rights needs on the Egegik drainage by 2007 and formally apply for them by 2009 (also Goal 1).

48. Complete water resource investigations and acquire water rights for waters identified in the water resource investigation plan (also Goal 1).

49. Continue limnological studies of Becharof and Ugashik lakes in cooperation with King Salmon Fisheries Research Office (also Goal 1).

50. Complete baseline water-quality studies of Refuges lakes and streams following the schedule identified in the water resources investigation plan (also Goal 1).

Goal 5: *Preserve and enhance, in perpetuity, wilderness values of designated Wilderness, consistent with the establishing purposes*

Objectives directed at the Becharof Wilderness Area are designed to manage and understand the wilderness values.

51. Distribute information about Leave-No-Trace principles whenever information is requested about the Becharof Wilderness Area, and work with commercial guides to apply these principles when operating within designated Wilderness.

52. By applying the Leave-No-Trace principles, manage recreation settings within designated Wilderness to provide opportunities for solitude, self-reliance, and other characteristics that depend on a wilderness environment while not impairing other uses and values associated with wilderness.

53. Promote consistency, through interagency coordination, in wilderness management of the Becharof Wilderness and the adjacent designated Wilderness of Katmai National Park and Preserve.

54. Ensure appropriate uses (including administrative uses) of the Becharof Wilderness on an ongoing basis by expanding law enforcement within designated Wilderness and conducting the minimum-requirement analysis to all management activities.

55. Prepare a wilderness stewardship step-down plan within one year of release of national wilderness guidelines.

Goal 6: *Provide opportunities for quality[1] wildlife-dependent recreation, emphasizing short-term, low-density uses that require minimal facility development or habitat alteration*

The National Wildlife Refuge System Administration Act of 1966, as amended by the National Wildlife Refuge System Improvement Act, states that compatible wildlife-dependent recreation is a legitimate and appropriate general public use of the System and directs the Service to facilitate hunting, fishing, wildlife viewing and photography, and environmental education and interpretation on refuges, subject to restrictions or regulations as needed. Objectives that are designed to address the resources necessary to support wildlife-dependent recreation are listed under Goal 2. Other objectives that help to provide high-quality experiences are described along with Goals 7 and 8. General management direction of public use on the Refuges, including commercial uses, is described in Section 4.

56. By continuing to implement and strengthen the Refuges special-use permit program—including improvement of permittee recording requirements—and increasing enforcement of and compliance with permit stipulations through increased field inspections, provide commercial visitor service opportunities for the public who would not or could not experience a safe, quality visit to the Refuges on their own (also Goal 8).

---

[1] Quality is defined as the degree to which recreation opportunities and related experiences meet the objectives for which they are planned and managed. For further definition of "quality" in relation to recreation, see the glossary in the Revised Comprehensive Conservation Plan and Environmental Impact Statement (October 2005).

Goal 7: *Provide opportunities for subsistence, recreational, and commercial users to enjoy and benefit from compatible activities on the Refuges in ways that minimize conflicts among user groups*

Section 804 of ANILCA states that subsistence will be the priority consumptive use of public lands in Alaska, consistent with the purposes for each unit. Fish and Wildlife Service policy describes quality recreation opportunities, in part, as creating minimal conflict with other wildlife-dependent recreation uses or refuge operations. The Refuges need to be aware of and address conflicts among refuge users. Many of the objectives in Goal 2 that consider harvest levels or monitor populations of fish and wildlife also provide important information for accomplishing this goal.

57. Expand the public-use monitoring program for all users of the Refuges. A special emphasis will be placed on annually monitoring all commercial-use activities and on establishing and/or expanding public-use monitoring camps on a scheduled basis at locations where potential exists for user conflicts, impacts, or declines in quality. A full-time, permanent pilot–resource manager position with collateral law enforcement duties, along with one or more seasonal positions, would be required to implement this objective (also Goals 6 and 8).

58. Field-check and update database of Alaska Native Claims Settlement Act (ANCSA) 17(b) easements, develop GIS maps of easements, establish signs onsite, and publish easement information as appropriate in coordination with realty specialists and local Native corporations (also Goal 6).

59. Expand profile of refuge law-enforcement activities. Law enforcement activities concerning protection of fish and wildlife resources will shift from patrols being conducted seasonally by collateral-duty refuge officers (typically incidental to other missions) to dedicated law-enforcement patrols being conducted year-round by a full-time refuge law-enforcement officer (also Goals 3 and 6).

Goal 8: *Conduct interpretive and environmental education programs that increase understanding and support for the System; development of a sense of stewardship for wildlife, cultural resources, and the environment; and enhanced visitor experiences*

60. Use the Refuge Information Technician program to conduct educational programs for local rural residents on resource conservation and protection, subsistence harvest developments, and recreational harvest management. Conduct at least one program per year in each of the 13 communities associated with the Refuges (also Goal 3).

61. Interpret Refuges resources and programs, provide educational material, and increase the quality of recreation experiences by fully implementing the interagency cooperative agreement to operate the King Salmon Visitor Center (KSVC), including maintaining responsibility for personnel and developing, upgrading, and maintaining permanent exhibits annually (also

Goal 6).

62. Increase local children's awareness of the Refuges, wildlife, and conservation by utilizing the Refuge Information Technician program to visit, at least once a semester during the school year, the 10 village schools in the Bristol Bay and Lake and the Peninsula boroughs that are within or near the Refuges' boundaries; provide the other seven schools in the Lake and Peninsula Borough with educational materials and programs at least three times a year (during National Wildlife Refuge Week and for the Goose Calendar contest). Continue to develop programs for National Fishing Week celebration, International Migratory Bird Day, and other special events.

63. Conduct the cooperatively sponsored Spirit of Becharof Lake Ecosystem Science Camp for 10–15 refuge-area high school students annually, with assistance from Refuge Information Technician program personnel.

64. Inform people about natural, cultural, and recreational resources and opportunities on the Refuges and their responsible use by developing and publishing at least one new or revised refuge-specific brochure annually and by maintaining a refuge Web site within one year of Plan approval (also Goals 6 and 7).

Goal 9: *Conserve the special geological and cultural values of the Refuges*

65. Conduct a paleontological inventory with emphasis on Jurassic sediments within Becharof Lake drainage, Ugashik Lakes drainage, and Black Lake drainage by 2010.

66. Continue cultural resources management in partnership with Native corporations, universities, museums, and others in accordance with the Cultural Resource Guide.

67. Continue to work with the Alaska Volcano Observatory to further our knowledge of the volcanic resources of the Refuges.

68. Administer and protect cultural resources so that the sites, buildings, structures, and objects of aesthetic and cultural value are preserved and maintained for scientific study and/or public appreciation (also Goal 8).

Goal 10: *Provide and maintain the facilities and equipment necessary to ensure a safe and secure environment for the visiting public and Service personnel*

Objectives for facilities management are directed at providing necessary buildings and other structures for administration of the Refuges in a safe manner.

69. Continue implementation of the administrative facility plan.

70. Continue an aggressive safety program.

71. Meet legal requirements for the administrative facilities of the Refuges (e.g., hazardous materials handling).

72. Establish a subheadquarters for the Chignik Unit by 2020.

73. Construct an administrative facility at the Yantarni Bay airstrip.

2.3 Management Policies and Guidelines

Some activities discussed here are not currently being conducted on the Refuges. For example, the discussion on threatened and endangered species would apply only if and when a listed species is known or thought to occur in the Refuges.

Although five management categories, ranging from Intensive Management to designated Wilderness, are used to describe management levels on National Wildlife Refuges in Alaska, only three management categories; Moderate Management, Minimal Management, and Wilderness are used to describe management levels on the Alaska Peninsula and Becharof Refuges. A management category is used to define the level of human activity appropriate to a specific area on a refuge. It is a set of refuge management directions applied to an area, in light of its resources and existing and potential uses, to facilitate management and the accomplishment of refuge purposes and goals. The Service could, in the future, designate refuge lands as Intensive Management through a plan amendment or revision. The Wilderness and Wild (and Scenic) River management categories are reserved for congressionally designated lands. The management activities table (Table 2) shows management activities for the three categories on these refuges.

Not all of the practices described in the following sections will apply to these refuges. See Table 2 for clarification; those activities that have gray backgrounds are not anticipated to apply to these refuges during the life of this Plan. Text pertaining to those activities is included for reference.

2.3.1 General

Management of the Refuges is governed by federal laws such as the National Wildlife Refuge System Administration Act of 1966 (Refuge Administration Act; 16 U.S.C. 668dd), as amended by the National Wildlife Refuge System Improvement Act of 1997 (Refuge Improvement Act; P.L. 105-57), and ANILCA; by regulations implementing these laws; by treaties; by Service policy; and by principles of sound resource management—which establish standards for resource management or limit the range of potential activities that may be allowed on the Refuges.

ANILCA authorizes traditional activities such as subsistence, the exercise of valid commercial fishing rights, hunting, fishing, and trapping in accordance with state and federal laws. Under Service regulations implementing this direction, all refuge lands in Alaska are open to public recreation activities "as long as such activities are conducted in a manner compatible with the purposes for which the refuge was established. Such recreation activities include sightseeing, nature observations and photography, sport hunting, sport fishing, boating, camping, hiking, picnicking and other related activities" (50 CFR 36.31[a]). The Refuge Administration Act, as amended by the National Wildlife Refuge System Improvement Act of 1997, defines "wildlife-dependent recreation" and "wildlife-dependent recreational use" as "hunting, fishing, wildlife observation and photography, or environmental education and interpretation" (16 U.S.C. § 668ee[2]). These uses are encouraged and will receive emphasis in management of the public's use of the Refuges.

2.3.2 Management Emergencies

It may be necessary, when emergencies occur on the refuge, to deviate from policies and guidelines discussed herein. Activities not allowed on the Refuges or under a specific management category, (as shown in Table 2), may occur during or as a result of emergencies. For example, if naturally occurring or human-caused actions (e.g., landslides, floods, fires, droughts) adversely affect refuge resources, it may be necessary to undertake rehabilitation, restoration, habitat improvement, water management, fisheries enhancement, or other actions that would not otherwise be allowed to the same extent on the refuge. Threats to human health and safety may also result during emergencies. In emergencies, the refuge manager is authorized to take prudent and reasonable actions to protect human life and to address immediate health, safety, or critical resource-protection needs.

2.3.3 Land Exchanges and Acquisitions

Under Section 1302 of ANILCA, and subject to certain restrictions, the Service may acquire by purchase, donation, or exchange any lands within the boundaries of Alaska refuges. Proposed land exchanges or acquisitions must benefit fish and wildlife resources, satisfy other purposes for which the refuge was established, or be necessary to satisfy other national interests. The Service can also purchase conservation easements or enter into cooperative management agreements to meet these objectives.

2.3.4 Land Protection Planning

Department of the Interior and Service policies require development of a step-down plan, a land protection plan, addressing priorities for habitat conservation within refuge boundaries. Land protection plans inform private landowners what land within refuge boundaries the Service would like to see conserved for fish and wildlife habitat. The plans do the following:

> Identify the private lands within the refuge boundary that the Service believes should be conserved

> Display the relative protection priority for each parcel

> Discuss alternative means of land and resource conservation

> Analyze the impacts, on local residents, of acquisition

In Alaska, the Service only acquires land from willing landowners. It is Service policy to acquire land only when other methods of achieving goals are not appropriate, available, or effective. Sometimes resource conservation goals can be met through cooperative management agreements with landowners or by similar means. The Refuges would work with all landowners to ensure that overall fish and wildlife and habitat values within the refuge are conserved.

A pre-acquisition environmental site assessment is required for all real property proposed for acquisition by the Service or for public domain lands returning to Service jurisdiction (USFWS, Part 341 FW 3).

The land protection plan for the Refuges was completed in 2002.

See also section 2.4 for discussion of stepdown plans.

2.3.5 Compatibility Determinations

The Refuge Administration Act states that "the Secretary is authorized, under such regulations as he [or she] may prescribe, to . . . permit the use of any area within the System for any purpose, including but not limited to hunting, fishing, public recreation and accommodations, and access whenever he [or she] determines that such uses are compatible . . . ."

A compatible use is a proposed or existing wildlife-dependent recreation use or any other use of a national wildlife refuge that, based on sound professional judgment, will not materially interfere with nor detract from the fulfillment of the National Wildlife Refuge System mission or the purposes for which the refuge was established. Economic uses must contribute to achieving refuge purposes and the System mission. Compatibility determinations are not required for refuge management activities, except economic activities.

If a use is found to be incompatible, the refuge would follow normal administrative procedures for stopping the action. If the use in question is a new use requiring a special use permit, the refuge manager would not issue a permit. If the use is an existing use already under permit, the refuge manager will work with the permittee to modify the use to make it compatible or would terminate the permit.

Ending incompatible uses that do not require special use permits or other formal authorizations, or that cannot be addressed by other federal or state agencies, would require that the refuge go through the normal rule-making process. This would include publishing in the Federal Register the proposed regulations and providing opportunity for public comment.

Compatibility determinations for uses on these Refuges are found in Appendix H of the Revised Comprehensive Conservation Plan and Environmental Impact Statement.

Compatibility determinations for existing hunting, fishing, wildlife observation and photography, and environmental education and interpretation must be re-evaluated with the preparation or revision of a Comprehensive Conservation Plan or at least every 15 years, whichever is earlier. Compatibility determinations for all other uses must be re-evaluated every 10 years or earlier if conditions change or significant new information relative to the use and its effects becomes available.

Additional details on applying compatibility standards and completing compatibility determinations are found in the compatibility regulations at 50 CFR Parts 25, 26, and 29 and Part 603 FW 2 of the Service Manual (USFWS).

2.3.6 Mitigation

In the interest of serving the public, it is the policy of the Service, throughout the nation, to seek to prevent, reduce, or compensate for losses of fish, wildlife, and their habitats, and uses thereof, from land and water development. To that end, the Service developed a "Mitigation Policy" in 1981 that includes measures ranging from avoiding an activity that results in loss of such resources to seeking compensation by replacement of or substitution for resource loss.

The Service will promulgate regulations, develop stipulations, and issue permits to reduce or eliminate potential adverse impacts resulting from compatible activities that may be authorized under this plan. These regulations, stipulations, and permits would mitigate impacts in a variety of means, as stipulated in the Mitigation Policy guidelines (USFWS, Part 501 FW 2.1). The means, in order of application, are as follows:

> Avoiding the impact altogether by not taking a certain action or parts of an action
>
> Minimizing impacts by limiting the degree or magnitude of the action and its implementation
>
> Rectifying the impact by repairing, rehabilitating, or restoring the affected environment
>
> Reducing or eliminating the impact over time by preservation and maintenance operations during the life of the action
>
> Compensating for the impact by replacing or providing substitute resources or environments

When determining the compatibility of activities or uses, consideration should be given to ways which the projects/activities/uses could be designed to avoid adverse impacts. The Service generally would not allow compensatory mitigation on System lands, and only in limited and exceptional circumstances could compensatory mitigation be used to find an activity compatible. (Service Manual, Part 501 FW 2 and 603 FW 2).

Mitigation may consist of standard stipulations such as those attached to right-of-way permits; special stipulations that may be attached to leases or permits on a site-specific basis; and site-specific, project-specific mitigation identified through detailed step-down management plans or the environmental assessment process. In all instances, mitigation must support the mission of the National Wildlife Refuge System and must be compatible with the purposes of the refuge. The degree, type, and extent of mitigation undertaken would depend on the site-specific conditions present and the management goals and objectives of the action being implemented.

2.3.7 Coastal Zone Consistency

Although federal lands, including lands in the National Wildlife Refuge System, are excluded from the coastal zone (16 U.S.C., Section 1453[1]), the Coastal Zone Management Act of 1972, as amended (PL 92-583), directs federal agencies conducting activities within the coastal zone or that may affect any land or water use or natural resources of the coastal zone to conduct these activities in a manner that is consistent "to the maximum extent practicable"[2] with approved state management programs.

The Alaska Coastal Zone Management Act of 1977, as amended, and the subsequent Alaska Coastal Management Program, as amended, and Final Environmental Impact Statement (1979) establish policy guidance and standards for the review of projects within or potentially affecting Alaska's coastal zone. In addition, specific policies have been developed for activities and uses of coastal lands and water resources within regional coastal resource districts. Most incorporated cities, municipalities, and boroughs as well as unincorporated areas (coastal resource service areas) within the coastal zone now have state-approved coastal management programs.

Although state and coastal district program policies are to guide consistency determinations, more restrictive federal agency standards may be applied. Federal regulations state that "(w)hen Federal agency standards are more restrictive than standards or requirements contained in the State's management program, the Federal agency may continue to apply its stricter standards . . ." (15 CFR, Section 930.39[d]).

Certain federal actions may require a Federal Coastal Consistency Determination. The Refuges will contact the Department of Natural Resources' Alaska Coastal Management Program with the Service's determination of consistency before beginning a project that may affect the coastal zone.

Section 7-1 of the Revised Comprehensive Conservation Plan and Environmental Impact Statement contains a consistency determination covering management of the Refuges.

2.3.8 Cooperation and Coordination with Others

2.3.8.1 Federal, State and Local Governments

The Refuges will continue to work closely with those federal, state, Native and local governments and agencies whose programs affect, or are affected by, the Refuges. State, local, and Native government inputs will be sought during development of regulatory policies addressing management of the Refuge System (Executive Order 13083—Federalism). When possible, the Service will participate in interagency activities (such as joint fish and wildlife surveys and co-funded

---

[2]   "To the maximum extent practicable" means, "to the fullest degree permitted by existing law (15 CFR, Section 930.32)."

research), cooperative agreements, sharing data, and sharing equipment and/or aircraft costs to meet mutual management goals and objectives.

When the Refuges are aware of issues involving management jurisdiction or authority over submerged lands or other areas, they will, under appropriate situations, coordinate with the State of Alaska. Coordination may involve formal and informal management agreements between the Service and the state, but the assertion of management authority will not be contingent on completing any agreements or any other action not required by federal law. Questions regarding the ownership of specific submerged lands may be addressed to the Refuges headquarters.

The Refuges and the State of Alaska will cooperatively manage the fish and wildlife resources of the Refuges. The Master Memorandum of Understanding between the Service and the Alaska Department of Fish & Game (dated March 13, 1982) defines the cooperative management roles of each agency (Appendix B of the Revised Comprehensive Conservation Plan and Environmental Impact Statement). In this agreement, the Alaska Department of Fish and Game agreed to "recognize the Service as the agency with the responsibility to manage migratory birds, endangered species, and other species mandated by Federal law, and on Service lands in Alaska to conserve fish and wildlife and their habitats and regulate human use." Correspondingly, the Service agreed to "recognize the right of the Alaska Department of Fish and Game as the agency with the primary responsibility to manage fish and resident wildlife within the State of Alaska." Further discussion of intergovernmental cooperation regarding the preservation, use, and management of fish and wildlife resources is found in Title 43 CFR, Part 24 (Department of the Interior Fish & Wildlife Policy: State and Federal Relationships).

We do not require compatibility determinations for state wildlife management activities on a national wildlife refuge pursuant to a cooperative agreement between the state and the Fish & Wildlife Service where the refuge manager has made a written determination that such activities support fulfilling the refuge purposes or the System mission. When the activity proposed by the state is not part of a cooperative agreement or it is not acting as the Service's agent, a special use permit may be required, and a compatibility determination will need to be completed before the activity may be allowed. Separate compatibility determinations addressing specific proposals will be required for state management activities that propose predator management, fish and wildlife control (with the exception of emergency removal of individual rogue animals), reintroduction of species, nonnative species management, pest management, disease prevention and control, fishery restoration, fishery enhancement, native fish introductions, nonnative species introductions, construction of facilities, helicopter access, or any other unpermitted activity that could alter refuge ecosystems.

2.3.8.2 Tribes and Native American Organizations

The Service's Native American Policy (USFWS 1994b) identifies general principles that guide the Service's government-to-government relationships with tribal governments in the conservation of fish and wildlife resources. Additional guidance has been provided by Executive Order 13084, "Consultation and Coordination with Indian Tribal Governments," issued May 14, 1998, and the Department of the Interior–Alaska Policy on Government-to-Government Relations with Alaska Native Tribes issued January 18, 2001 (USDI 2001). The Refuges will maintain government-to-government relationships with tribal governments. The Refuges will also work directly with regional and village corporations and respect Native American cultural values when planning and implementing programs on the refuges.

2.3.8.3 Owners of Refuge Inholdings and Adjacent Lands

The Refuges will work cooperatively with inholders and adjacent landowners, providing information on refuge management activities and policies. The Refuges will consult periodically with them regarding topics of mutual interest; will respond promptly to concerns over refuge programs; and will participate in cooperative projects (e.g., water-quality monitoring and fish and wildlife management).

2.3.8.4 Service Jurisdiction Over Waters Within the Refuges

Where the United States holds title to submerged lands beneath waters within the Alaska Peninsula National Wildlife Refuge and the Becharof National Wildlife Refuge, the Service has jurisdiction over activities on the water. The Service's statutory authority to manage these lands and waters comes from the National Wildlife Refuge System Administration Act of 1966, as amended, and the Alaska National Interest Conservation Act (ANILCA). Under provisions of ANILCA, the Service manages the federal subsistence program on all waters within and adjacent to the external boundaries of the Refuges.

In 1980, under ANILCA, the U.S. Congress established the Alaska Peninsula and Becharof National Wildlife Refuges. These areas of land and water may contain both navigable and nonnavigable waters. Where waterbodies are nonnavigable within the Refuges, the Service has management authority over activities on water where adjacent uplands are federally owned. Where State of Alaska lands exist beneath navigable waterbodies or where the state, a Native corporation, or a Native allotee owns the adjacent uplands within areas of the ANILCA-established Refuges, the Service's management authority is limited.

2.3.8.5 Other Constituencies

The Refuges will inform local communities, special interest groups, and others who have expressed an interest in or are affected by refuge programs about refuge management policies and activities. The Refuges will seek input from these constituents when issues arise that may affect how the refuge is managed. Whenever possible, local residents and special interest groups will be asked to participate in refuge activities so their expertise and local knowledge can be incorporated into refuge management.

2.3.9 Ecosystem and Landscape Management

Species do not function alone; they function together in the environment as part of an ecosystem. The Refuges will employ ecosystem-management techniques in resource management of the Refuges. Individual species are viewed as integral to the diversity of those ecosystems and as such are indicators of the healthy functioning of the entire ecosystem. When the Service identifies species to use as indicators of the health of the ecosystem, it will do so through a rigorous peer-reviewed scientific process involving experts from other federal agencies and the Alaska Department of Fish & Game.

Inventorying, monitoring, and maintaining a comprehensive database of selected ecosystem components is critical for making refuge management decisions and for ensuring the proper long-term stewardship of refuge ecosystems. This includes regular and recurring monitoring of status and trends for ecosystem components such as fish, wildlife, plants, climatic conditions, soils, and waterbodies. All monitoring will employ appropriate disciplines, new technologies, and scientific capabilities whenever practical.

2.3.9.1 Air Quality

The Service's authorities for air-quality management are included in several laws. The most direct mandates to manage air resources are found in the Wilderness Act and the Clean Air Act.

The Service is required by the Clean Air Act to preserve, protect, and enhance air quality and air quality–related values on Service lands. Air quality–related values include visibility, plants, animals, soil, water quality, cultural and historical resources, and virtually all resources that are dependent upon and affected by air quality. In addition, the Wilderness Act requires the Service to protect and preserve the Wilderness character, including the pristine air quality, of designated areas.

Class I air-quality sites receive the highest level of protection. Very little deterioration is allowed in these areas, and the federal land manager has an "affirmative responsibility" to protect air quality–related values on those lands. With the exception of three Class I air-quality sites in designated Wilderness on the Alaska Maritime National Wildlife Refuge, all other lands managed by the Service in Alaska are classified as Class II and receive protection through the Clean Air Act. Moderate deterioration, associated with well-managed growth, is allowed in Class II areas.

If air quality or related resources are at risk, the refuge manager will work with the Service's Air Quality Branch; the Regional air quality coordinator; the Alaska Department of Environmental Conservation and other state, local, and federal agencies and the public, as appropriate, in developing an air-quality management plan as outlined in the Service Manual, Part 563, FW 2.8 (USFWS).

2.3.9.2 Water Resources Management

Every national wildlife refuge in Alaska shares the common purpose of ensuring that water resources are maintained and protected. ANILCA mandates that the Service safeguard water quality and necessary water quantity within the Refuges.

Although the Service has reserved water rights sufficient to accomplish the purposes of the Refuges, the National Wildlife Refuge System Administration Act (16 USC 660dd) and the Service Manual (403 FW 1-3) direct the Service to obtain, to the extent practicable, water supplies of adequate quantity and quality for Service facilities, for refuge purposes and as trust resources, and to obtain the legal right to use that water through state laws, regulations, and procedures.

The Alaska Region conducted a water-resources threats analysis (Harle 1994) for the purpose of guiding water resource investigations and protecting water resources by acquiring instream-water-rights protection. Based on the results of the threats analysis, the Service's Regional Office developed a strategic plan for systematically quantifying the surface water on refuges within Alaska (Bayha *et al.* 1997).

Using existing data, or through the collection of hydrologic and biologic data, the Service applies to the State of Alaska for appropriative water rights, for instream water reservations, and for water withdrawals to meet the purposes identified in ANILCA and the Refuge System Improvement Act.

Establishing state water rights is only a part of a management strategy to protect refuge resources and to understand ecosystem processes. Collection of hydrologic data allows the Service to accomplish the following:

Plan flood-plain and riparian zone management

Estimate flow for ungauged refuge streams

Supplement historical or current fisheries and wildlife studies

Detect and evaluate future natural or human-induced changes in the hydrologic system

Provide stream profile and velocity data for the design of fish weirs or other structures

Estimate the potential for future flooding and erosion

Analyze the impacts of proposed projects on stream flow and water supply

> Provide a basis for decision-making about commercial operations on some important streams

All facilities and activities on refuges must comply with pollution-control standards set by Federal laws (e.g., the Clean Water Act [33 U.S.C. 1251] and the Safe Drinking Water Act [42 U.S.C. 300]), state laws where federal law so provides, and the regulations, policies, and standards implementing these laws.

2.3.9.3 Visual Resource Management

Visual resource management has two primary purposes: (1) to manage the quality of the visual environment and (2) to reduce the visual impact of development activities. To accomplish these purposes, the Refuges will identify and maintain the scenic values of the refuge and will, within the constraints imposed by the conservation plan, minimize the visual impacts of development and use of the refuge. All activities and facilities on the Refuges will be designed to blend into the landscape to the extent practical. The Service will cooperate with other federal, state, local, tribal, and private agencies and organizations to prevent significant deterioration of visual resources.

2.3.9.4 Cultural, Historical, and Paleontological Resources

The Service has long-term responsibilities for cultural resources on refuge lands. Cultural resources on refuge lands are managed under a number of laws, executive orders, and regulations, including the Antiquities Act; the National Historic Preservation Act, as amended; the Archaeological Resources Protection Act; the American Indian Religious Freedom Act; the Native American Graves Protection and Repatriation Act; Executive Order 11593, Protection and Enhancement of the Cultural Environment; Executive Order 13007, Indian Sacred Sites; and Section 36 of the Code of Federal Regulations, Part 800.

The 1980 amendments to the National Historic Preservation Act direct the Service to inventory and evaluate cultural resources for their eligibility for inclusion on the National Register of Historic Places. All significant historic, archaeological, cultural, and paleontological resources on the refuge will be protected and managed in accordance with federal and state law. Because of limits of time, funding, and staffing, the Service must designate priorities in evaluating cultural resources on refuge lands. Pending a complete evaluation, all cultural resources will be considered potentially eligible for the National Register. Sites determined to be eligible for the National Register will be protected with a cultural resources management plan.

The cultural resource guide for the Refuges was completed in 1996 and is scheduled to be updated in 2008. It provides guidance for cultural resource management on the Refuges by outlining legal mandates and considerations, reviewing current information about the resources, and establishing goals and objectives for the program. (Also see cultural resource guides in the step-down plans section.)

It is illegal to collect archaeological materials and/or vertebrate paleontological remains on the Refuges without a permit issued under the provisions of the Archaeological Resources Protection Act (for archaeological materials) or of the Antiquities Act of 1906 (vertebrate paleontological remains). Historic aircraft and other World War II material will be managed in accordance with a policy published December 20, 1985, in the Federal Register (FR 50:51952-51953). These materials may be collected on refuge lands only as authorized by a permit issued to a qualified organization or individual. Cultural resource research permits will only be issued to qualified individuals operating under appropriate research designs. The Refuges will encourage archaeologists, historians, ethnologists, and paleontologists from educational institutions and other government agencies to pursue their research interests on refuge lands so long as these research interests are compatible with refuge purposes. Research that collects data from threatened sites and minimizes disturbance to intact sites will be encouraged.

When any federal undertaking—including any action funded or authorized by the federal government and having the potential to directly or indirectly affect any archaeological or historic site—is planned, a consultation must be initiated with the State Historic Preservation Officer, under Section 106 of the National Historic Preservation Act. If sites that may be affected are found in the project area, their significance will be evaluated to determine their eligibility for inclusion in the National Register. For eligible sites, consultation will result in a course of action causing the least possible impact. Impacts may be minimized in a variety of ways, including relocation or redesign of a project, site hardening, mitigation through information collection, or cancellation of the project if no alternatives are feasible. To protect archaeological and historic sites, other uses may be precluded. Private interests proposing to conduct commercial uses on the refuge will normally be required to fund studies necessary for consultation and for mitigation of impacts.

The Refuges will implement Executive Order 13007, Indian Sacred Sites, allowing access to identified sacred sites and avoiding adversely affecting the physical integrity of these sites. Where appropriate, the Service will maintain the confidentiality of sacred sites.

Further information on cultural resources management can be found in Part 614 FW 1, 2, 3, 4 and 5 of the Service Manual and the Service's Cultural Resources Management Handbook (USFWS 1992).

2.3.10 Fish and Wildlife Habitat Management
2.3.10.1 Habitat Management

Habitats are managed in keeping with the purposes, goals, and objectives of a refuge. In most cases, this means habitats are managed to maintain a natural state with little or no human intervention. In some cases, habitats are manipulated to maintain or improve conditions for selected fish and wildlife populations, to control plant species, or to manage fire fuels on refuge lands. Any habitat management and manipulation activities will be carried out in support of the purposes, goals, and objectives of the Refuges. The Refuges will use the least-intrusive management measures needed. Where practical and economically feasible, habitat management practices will maintain a natural appearance on the landscape. Habitat-management practices, even those carried out for the benefit of a single species or small group of species, will, to the extent possible, contribute to the widest diversity of native (indigenous) wildlife species and habitat types.

Habitat management and manipulation may be achieved by mechanical or manual methods, or by a combination of methods. Mechanical treatment could include mechanical removal, crushing, cutting, or mowing. Mechanical treatment could also include the construction of fish passages, fish ladders, fish barriers, water impoundments and structures such as fences or artificial nests, and raising or lowering of water levels to manage wildlife or waterfowl habitat. Riparian or aquatic habitat management and manipulation may be achieved by acquiring instream-flow reservations or making beneficial water diversions.

Chemical treatment would involve the use of chemicals to restore nutrient levels in a lake system (fertilization) for fisheries restoration, to reduce hazardous fuels, or to eliminate nonnative plant and animal species, normally by killing them or destroying their ability to spread or prosper. Before chemical treatment is used, the Refuges will analyze the need for action, the options for treatment, and the potential impacts of those options. A pesticide-use proposal must be approved by the Service's Regional Office before chemical controls are used on refuge lands (30 AM 12 and 7 RM 14).

Manual treatment could include the use of hand tools to remove, reduce, or modify hazardous fuels or nonnative plant or animal species or to modify habitats (e.g., removal of beaver dams).

Aquatic habitat modification may include activities and structures such as streambank restoration, passage structures, and removal of fish barriers or obstacles that results in physical modification of aquatic or riparian habitats to benefit fish species. These activities would be undertaken to maintain or restore native fish populations and may require appropriate National Environmental Policy Act (NEPA) compliance and compatibility determinations.

2.3.10.2 Fire Management

The Refuges are exempt from developing a fire management plan because of the low incidence of wildland fires.

Wildland Fire Suppression

Fire suppression activity is the work of confining, constraining, controlling, or monitoring a fire or portion of a fire to protect, prevent, or reduce the loss of identified values. Suppression takes place, with the highest priority being the safety of firefighters and the public, using the appropriate management response based on values to be protected. The

Alaska Interagency Wildland Fire Management Plan, amended in October 1998, is the guiding document for suppression actions. The plan establishes four management options—critical, full, modified, and limited—that direct a range of wildlife fire management responses.

The Bureau of Land Management—Alaska Fire Service (BLM/AFS) provides emergency suppression services on refuge lands in Alaska (DOI 2001, DM 2), as directed by the refuge manager. Through a cooperative agreement with BLM/AFS, the State of Alaska Division of Forestry provides emergency suppression services on refuge lands in state protection zones, as directed by the refuge manager.

Wildland Fire Use

Wildland fire use is the application of the appropriate management response to naturally ignited wildland fires to accomplish resource management objectives outlined in fire management plans. Wildland fires may be used to protect, maintain, and enhance natural and cultural resources and, as nearly as possible, wildland fires will be allowed to function in their natural ecological role

Prescribed Fire

Prescribed fires are ignited by management action to meet specific wildland fuel, vegetation, and habitat management objectives. Prior to each ignition, a written, approved plan outlining prescription conditions is required. Use of prescribed fires must comply with the Alaska Enhanced Smoke Management Plan for Prescribed Fire. This plan provides guidance and direction concerning smoke issues related to prescribed fire.

2.3.10.3 Weed Control (Pest and Nonnative Plant Management)

Weeds can cause significant impacts to the land and water resources and to the species of plants and animals that use these habitats. To manage weeds, the Refuges will include weed inventories as part of all habitat inventories. The Refuges will review a proposed action's potential to introduce or spread weeds and will take measures to reduce the hazards (e.g., require weed-free feed for pack animals). The Refuges will coordinate with other landowners and agencies and use integrated pest-management practices to enhance the detection, prevention, and management of weed problems. Use of chemical control measures on refuge lands requires Regional Office approval of a pesticide-use proposal (30 AM 12 and 7 RM 14).

2.3.11 Fish and Wildlife Population Management

Conservation of habitat is a key element in maintaining the natural diversity of populations on the Refuges, and management of native fish and wildlife populations is an important component of maintaining a healthy ecosystem. The Refuges will be managed consistent with the Policy on Maintaining Biological Integrity, Diversity, and Environmental Health of the National Wildlife Refuge System (USFWS, 601 FW 3) to ensure native species are managed in their natural diversity and abundance.

The Refuges will work with the State of Alaska to conserve fish and wildlife populations, recognizing that populations may experience fluctuations in abundance because of environmental factors and may require management actions for conservation purposes. The Refuges will be managed to maintain the genetic variability of wild, native fish stocks.

2.3.11.1 Wildlife Inventory and Monitoring Plan

To assess presence, relative abundance, distribution, and trends in populations of fish, wildlife, and plants, the Refuges will draft a wildlife inventory and monitoring (I&M) plan. This is a step down plan which describes objectives, justification, methods, management implications, geographic scale, report schedules, and database management for studies on species targeted for inventory and monitoring. The I&M plan will include studies that address environmental parameters (e.g., weather) and hydrology, soils, and fire history to explain potential changes in the distribution, relative abundance, and populations of fish, wildlife, and plants. The I&M plan will be forwarded to the Service's Regional Office for review by the regional refuge biologist and other professional staff prior to final approval by the regional refuge chief. The Refuges will update their I&M plan on an annual basis but will only need regional review and approval every five years.

2.3.11.2 Scientific Peer Review

Biologists, ecologists, botanists, and other refuge personnel conducting scientific investigations will adhere to refuge, regional, Service, and Department of Interior policies on scientific conduct, including scientific peer review. The overall goal of scientific peer review is to ensure that information collected, analyzed, interpreted, and reported to the public and upon which policy and management decisions are based, meets established standards of the scientific community. To achieve this goal, refuge biologists, ecologists, botanists, and others serving as principal investigators will write a study plan that will undergo peer review. In addition, study plans, reports, and manuscripts that summarize the results of scientific studies, analyses, assessments, or syntheses developed by, or supported by, the Service will undergo scientific review prior to publication. The type and level of review shall be commensurate with the potential significance of the scientific information and its likely influence on policy and management actions.

2.3.11.3 Compliance with the Animal Welfare Act

The Animal Welfare Act of 1996 established legal standards for animal care and use. To prescribe methods and set standards for the design, performance, and conduct of animal care and use, research facilities and federal agencies must establish an Institutional Animal Care and Use Committee (IACUC). Field studies conducted or authorized by refuge employees within the purview of the Animal Welfare Act will require review and approval of an IACUC. Any refuge study that involves an invasive procedure or that harms or materially alters the behavior of an animal under study should be reviewed and approved by the Fish & Wildlife Service's (Region 7) IACUC prior to implementing fieldwork.

2.3.11.4 Marking and Banding

These activities include fish and wildlife capture, marking, banding, radio-collaring, release, tracking, and other information-gathering techniques. Cooperation with appropriate partners, including the Alaska Department of Fish & Game, will be stressed, and specific protocols will be followed, taking advantage of all appropriate disciplines and new technologies wherever possible.

2.3.11.5 Threatened or Endangered Species

The Refuges will consult with the U.S. Fish & Wildlife Service Ecological Services field office on actions that may affect listed, proposed, or candidate species or designated or proposed critical habitat. These actions include refuge operations, public-use programs, private lands and Federal Aid activities, promulgating regulations, and issuing permits (USFWS 1973, Section 7, Consultation Handbook 1998).

2.3.11.6 Introductions and Reintroductions

A species may be introduced on a refuge only if that species is native to the refuge (i.e., a reintroduction). Nonnative species may not be introduced. Definitions of native and nonnative species are found in the glossary of the Revised Comprehensive Conservation Plan and Environmental Impact Statement.

Reintroductions can be useful tools for restoring species to natural ranges and reestablishing a refuge's natural fish, wildlife, and habitat diversity. Reintroductions would require appropriate NEPA compliance, a review to ensure consistency with the biological integrity policy, an ANILCA Section 810 subsistence determination, and a refuge compatibility determination. Reintroductions also require extensive coordination with adjacent landowners and with the State of Alaska. In evaluating the project, the cause(s) of the extirpation[3] should be evaluated and management actions taken to alleviate the cause(s) prior to reintroduction.

The environmental requirements of the species and the ecological dynamics of the area proposed for the reintroduction need to be thoroughly reviewed prior to a reintroduction. Some factors to consider include behavior, diseases, general ecology of the species, habitat requirements, inter- and intra-species competition, life history, genetics, management practices, population dynamics, and predators. Consideration should be given to whether there have been significant habitat changes since extirpation of the species (e.g., is the area still within the species' natural range?).

---

[3] localized extinction of a species

2.3.11.7 Fish and Wildlife Control

These activities involve the control, relocation, and/or removal of native species, including predators, to maintain natural diversity of fish, wildlife, and habitats. These management actions may be employed with species of fish and wildlife within their original range to restore other depleted native populations. These activities are subject to appropriate NEPA compliance, an ANILCA Section 810 subsistence determination, and a refuge compatibility determination.

Predator management includes the relocation, removal, sterilization, and other management of native predators to accomplish management objectives. The Service considers predator management to be a legitimate conservation tool when applied in a prudent and ecologically sound manner and when other alternatives are not practical. The key requirements are that a predator-management program be ecologically sound and biologically justified. In keeping with the Service's mandate to first and foremost maintain the biological integrity, diversity, and environmental health of fish and wildlife populations at the refuge scale, a predator population will not intentionally be reduced below a level consistent with the low-end of natural population cycles (see 601 FW 3).

A predator-management program requires appropriate NEPA compliance, an ANILCA Section 810 subsistence evaluation, and, if conducted by other than the Service, a refuge compatibility determination. Alternative management actions must be evaluated prior to pursuing direct predator-control activities. Any proposal to allow or implement a predator-management program on national wildlife refuges in Alaska will be subjected to public review and closely coordinated with the Alaska Department of Fish & Game, local communities, tribal governments, and adjacent landowners and/or managers. Predator-management activities must be monitored and evaluated for effectiveness and resource impacts.

Normal environmental education and population-management activities—such as trapper education programs and regulation changes that allow for increased harvests of predatory animals by licensed trappers and hunters—are not considered to be "predator management." The control or extirpation of nonnative predators is not considered to be "predator management" (see Section 2.3.11.8).

2.3.11.8 Nonnative Species Management

In general, nonnative species (including feral domestic animals) are not compatible with refuge purposes or with National Wildlife Refuge System policies. When nonnative species (fish, wildlife, or plants) occur on a refuge, the Service may control or eliminate that species. Where a population of a nonnative species has already been established on a refuge and this population does not materially interfere with or detract from the fulfillment of the mission of the National Wildlife Refuge System or the purposes of the refuge, the species may be managed as part of the refuge's diverse ecosystem.

2.3.11.9 Fish and Wildlife Pest Management and Disease Prevention and Control

Organisms (e.g., rabies or parasites) that threaten human health and property or survival of native wildlife or plant species may be managed or removed after consideration of all reasonable options and consultation with the State of Alaska and other concerned parties. This will normally only occur when severe resource damage is likely or when public health or safety is jeopardized. Wherever possible, an integrated approach to pest management will be used in accordance with the U.S. Fish & Wildlife Service Administrative Manual, 30 AM 12 and 7 RM 14. If chemical controls are used, a pesticide-use proposal must be submitted to the Service's Regional Office for approval.

2.3.11.10 Fishery Restoration

Fishery restoration is any management action that increases fishery resources to allow full use of available habitat or to reach a population level based on historical biologic data. Although the goal of restoration is self-sustaining populations, situations may exist in which some form of fishery management or facilities could continue indefinitely.

Where fishery resources have been severely adversely affected, the Refuge will work with the State of Alaska, local tribes, and other partners to restore habitats and populations to appropriate, sustainable conditions. Restoration emphasis will focus on strategies that are the least intrusive to the ecosystem and that do not compromise the viability or genetic characteristics of the depleted population. This may include regulatory adjustments and/or evaluations of escapement goals. If the stocks have been reduced or are threatened, temporary restoration facilities may be allowed in designated Wilderness, as long as the facilities will not significantly detract from the values for which those areas were established.

2.3.11.11 Fishery Enhancement

Fishery enhancement is any management action or set of actions that is applied to a fishery stock to supplement numbers of harvestable fish to a level beyond that which could be naturally produced based on a determination or reasonable estimate of historic levels. This could be accomplished by stocking barren lakes, providing access to barren spawning areas (fish passages), constructing hatcheries, outstocking in productive systems, or fertilizing rearing habitat.

Refuge management priorities will focus on conserving naturally diverse ecosystems. Fishery-enhancement facilities for the purposes of artificially increasing fish populations normally will not occur within any management category unless stocks have been reduced or are threatened.

Proposals for fishery-enhancement projects will be subject to the provisions of NEPA, an ANILCA Section 810 subsistence determination, and a compatibility determination. Only temporary fisheries-enhancement facilities may be authorized in Minimal and Wilderness management areas. Proposals for facilities within designated Wilderness require a minimum-requirements analysis to determine if the facilities are necessary within the Wilderness area and would not significantly detract from the values for which those areas were established.

2.3.11.12   *Fish Management Planning*

The Refuges Fishery Management Plan is scheduled for revision in 2008. This plan provides additional guidance on information needs and on management actions needed on the Refuges. The Service would involve partners (e.g., State of Alaska and local tribes) in the revision process.

2.3.12   *Subsistence Use Management*

Providing the opportunity for continued subsistence use by local residents is one of the purposes of these refuges, as stated in Title III Sections 302 (1)(B) and (2)(B) and Section 303 (1)(B) of ANILCA. Title VIII of ANILCA further provides that rural Alaska residents engaged in subsistence use of resources be allowed to continue using refuge resources for traditional purposes. These resources include fish and wildlife, house logs and firewood, and other plant materials (berries, bark, etc.).

Many aspects of subsistence management are addressed outside of this plan. The Federal Subsistence Board, through its rule-making process, addresses seasons, harvest limits, and customary and traditional use determinations. This board has established regional advisory councils to provide for meaningful public input to the rule-making process.

The Refuges will work with others to monitor subsistence harvest, including monitoring conducted by other federal land management agencies, the State of Alaska, tribal governments, Native organizations, or any other party. The Refuges will supplement the state's ongoing harvest and resource monitoring programs to provide additional information on the status of fish and wildlife populations harvested for subsistence uses. This monitoring is intended to identify potential problems before populations of fish and wildlife become depleted and to ensure preference is given to subsistence users as required by law. All information the refuge gathers through subsistence monitoring will be shared with local state fish and game advisory committees, tribes, and other entities. Refuge staff members attend various subsistence-related meetings, including those of local fish and game advisory committees and Regional Subsistence Advisory Councils and provides information on the status of subsistence resources and management as they relate to the Refuges.

The noncommercial gathering by local rural residents of fruits, berries, mushrooms, and other plant materials for subsistence uses and of dead standing or down timber for firewood is allowed without a special use permit. Harvest of live standing timber for house logs, firewood, or other uses is allowed, although specific requirements vary by size and location. See 50 CFR 36.15 (U.S. Government 1996-2003) for specific details. Timber stocks subject to subsistence use will also be monitored to ensure they remain available over the long term.

Under Section 816 of ANILCA, refuge lands may be closed to the taking of fish and wildlife if closure is deemed necessary for reasons of public safety, administration, or to ensure the continued viability of particular populations of fish or wildlife. Emergency closure to subsistence taking generally would occur only after other consumptive uses competing for the resources were restricted or eliminated.

2.3.12.1 Access for Subsistence Purposes

Access to refuge lands by traditional means will be allowed for subsistence purposes in accordance with Section 811 of ANILCA, subject to reasonable regulation (see 50 CFR 36.12). Traditional means include snowmachines, motorboats, dog teams, and other means of surface transportation traditionally used by local rural residents engaged in subsistence activities. Use of these traditional means of travel will be in compliance with state and federal law in such a manner to prevent waste of harvested resources or damage to the refuge and to prevent herding, harassment, hazing, or driving of wildlife.

As specified in 50 CFR 36.39(c), three- and four-wheeled vehicles with a maximum gross vehicle weight of 650 pounds are allowed on the Refuges for subsistence purposes.

2.3.12.2 Section 810 Evaluations

The Refuges will evaluate the effects of proposed activities on subsistence use to ensure compliance with Section 810 of ANILCA. The Refuges will work with the Federal Subsistence Board, regional subsistence advisory councils, local fish and game advisory committees, tribes, Native corporations, the Alaska Department of Fish & Game, and other appropriate local sources to determine whether a proposed activity would "significantly restrict" subsistence uses. If the Refuges determine that a proposal would probably result in adverse effects to subsistence use, the Refuges would follow the requirements identified in Section 810 before making a final decision on the proposal.

2.3.13 Public Access and Transportation Management

2.3.13.1 Snowmachines, Motorboats, Airplanes, and Nonmotorized Surface Transportation

Section 1110(a) of ANILCA allows the use of snowmachines (during periods of adequate snow cover and frozen river conditions), motorboats, airplanes, and nonmotorized surface transportation methods for traditional activities and for travel to and from villages and homesites. Such access shall be subject to reasonable regulations to protect natural and other values of the refuge (43 CFR 36.11). Specific areas may be closed, in accordance with these regulations, to such uses. The refuge manager is responsible for determining when snow cover is adequate to protect the underlying vegetation and soil from damage by snowmachine use.

2.3.13.2 Helicopters and Off-Road Vehicles

The regulations in 43 CFR 36.11 restrict use of helicopters and off-road vehicles.

Off-Road Vehicles

The regulations in 43 CRF 36.11(g) restrict the use of off-road vehicles within refuges. The definition of off-road vehicles in 50 CFR 36.2 excludes snowmachines but includes air boats and air-cushion vehicles along with motorized wheeled vehicles. Under 50 CFR 36.39 (c), off-road vehicles are allowed only on designated routes or areas within the Yantarni Bay Moderate Management area or by special use permit. (Provisions have been made for the use of off-road vehicles for subsistence purposes, see section 2.3.12.1.)

Helicopters

Special use permits or other authorizations are required for all helicopter landings in any place other than at designated landing areas. Exceptions include emergencies, search and rescue operations, or operations conducted by the Service (43 CFR 36.11(f)(4).

Helicopter landings for volcano monitoring, geologic hazards evaluations, and fisheries and wildlife management activities may be authorized under special use permit or other authorization, subject to site-specific stipulations. Helicopter landings for initial-attack fire suppression must comply with operational guidance in the Alaska Interagency Wildland Fire Management Plan. Helicopter landings by commercial operators and for general public access are not allowed in designated Wilderness unless the use was established prior to designation.

2.3.13.3 Access to Inholdings

Section 1110(b) of ANILCA ensures adequate and feasible access, for economic or other purposes, across a refuge for any person or entity who has a valid inholding. An inholding is defined as state-owned or privately owned land, including subsurface rights underlying public lands, valid mining claims, or other valid occupancy that is within or effectively surrounded by one or more conservation system units. When a right-of-way permit is necessary under this provision (e.g., construction of permanent or long-term facilities), the Service will review and process the application in accordance with regulations in 43 CFR 36.5, 36.6 and 50 CFR 29.21. Such permits are subject to terms and conditions as specified in the regulations at 43 CFR 36.9 and 50 CFR 29.21-4.

2.3.13.4 Temporary Access

43 CFR 36.12(a)(2) defines temporary access as limited, short-term (i.e., up to one year from issuance of the permit) access that does not require permanent facilities and for access to state or private lands. Temporary access is limited to survey, geophysical, exploratory, or similar temporary uses of nonfederal lands.

The Refuges will evaluate applications for temporary access across the Refuges and shall issue a permit with the necessary stipulations and conditions to ensure that the access granted is compatible with the purposes for which the refuges were established, that it complies with the provisions of Section 810 of ANILCA, and that it ensures that no permanent harm will result to the resources of the Refuges.

2.3.13.5 Subsistence Access

See Access for Subsistence Purposes under Subsistence Use Management (section 2.3.12.1).

2.3.13.6 Transportation and Utility Systems

Transportation and utility systems include roads, highways, railroads, airports, pipelines, electrical transmission lines, communication systems, and related structures and facilities reasonably and minimally necessary for the construction, operation, and maintenance of such systems (Section 1102 of ANILCA). Anyone seeking to acquire a right-of-way across refuge lands for a transportation or utility system must, consistent with 43 CFR Part 36, file an application with the Service's Regional Office. Regulations in 43 CFR Part 36 and 50 CFR Part 29 establish specific procedures and time constraints for application review, compliance with the National Environmental Policy Act, decision-making, and appeals.

The Service will decide whether to approve or disapprove that portion of a transportation or utility system that would cross refuge lands, except for those on designated Wilderness. When the proposed transportation or utility system would cross a designated Wilderness area, the Service tentatively approves or disapproves the application subject to the President's subsequent decision. If the President approves, a recommendation is submitted to Congress for final approval.

A right-of-way for a transportation or utility system across refuge lands can be granted only if the system meets the compatibility standard, the criteria outlined in Section 1104(g)(2) of ANILCA, and the regulations at 43 CFR 36.7(a)(2) and if there is no economically feasible and prudent alternative route for the system. If approved, permits issued for a transportation or utility system will contain terms and conditions as required under regulations in 43 CFR 36.9(b) and 50 CFR 29.21-4. Additional special requirements apply to rights-of-way for pipelines issued under the Mineral Leasing Act of 1920, 30 U.S.C. 185 (Section 1107[c] of ANILCA and the regulations at 43 CFR 36.9[d]).

For cases in which a transportation or utility system is proposed to cross areas in management categories that do not allow those systems, the authorization process would include consideration of a corresponding plan amendment.

2.3.13.7 State Transportation Planning

Federal transportation planning regulations require each state to develop a long-range statewide transportation plan in consultation and coordination with other government agencies and the public. In Alaska, transportation projects nominated for funding are evaluated and ranked by the Alaska Department of Transportation and Public Facilities. When appropriate, the refuge will participate in the state transportation-planning process and provide input regarding environmental considerations of proposed projects affecting refuge lands and resources. See Appendix G of the Revised Comprehensive Conservation Plan and Environmental Impact Statement for a discussion of state-identified potential transportation and utility systems that cross Refuge lands.

2.3.13.8 RS 2477 Rights-of-Way

The State of Alaska asserts numerous claims to roads, trails, and paths across federal lands under Revised Statute 2477 (RS 2477), a section in the Mining Act of 1866 that states, "The right-of-way for the construction of highways over public lands, not reserved for public uses, is hereby granted." RS 2477 was repealed by the Federal Land Policy and Management Act of 1976, subject to valid existing claims.

Assertion and identification of potential rights-of-way does not establish the existence of these claims nor the public's right to use them. The existence of all RS 2477 rights-of-way will be determined on a case-by-case basis, either through the courts or by other legally binding document.

Appendix B: Easements, Withdrawals, and Asserted Rights of Way and Figure 10: Asserted RS-2477 Routes present these asserted rights-of-way.

2.3.13.9 Section 17(b) Easements

Section 17(b) of the Alaska Native Claims Settlement Act of December 18, 1971, authorizes the Secretary of the Interior to reserve easements on lands conveyed to Native corporations to guarantee access to public lands and waters. Easements across Native lands include linear easements (e.g., roads and trails) and site easements. Site easements are reserved for use as temporary campsites and to change modes of transportation.

The Service is responsible for administering those public easements, inside and outside of refuge boundaries, which provide access to refuge lands. Service authority for administering 17(b) easements is restricted to the lands within the easement. The size, route, and general location of 17(b) easements are identified on maps filed with conveyance documents. Conveyance documents also specify the terms and conditions of use, including the acceptable periods and methods of public access.

2.3.13.10 Navigation Aids and Other Facilities

Section 1310 of ANILCA authorizes reasonable access to and operation and maintenance of existing air and water navigation aids, communications sites, and related facilities. It authorizes existing facilities for weather, climate, and fisheries research and monitoring subject to applicable laws and regulations. Reasonable access to and operation and maintenance of facilities for national defense and related air and water navigation are also provided for, including within designated Wilderness Areas.

New facilities may be authorized after consultation with the head of the federal department or agency undertaking the establishment, operation, or maintenance and in accordance with mutually agreed to terms and conditions.

2.3.14 Recreation and Other Public Use

Public recreation activities compatible with refuge purposes are authorized unless specifically prohibited (50 CFR 36.31). Compatible recreation uses of the refuge will continue. The Refuge Administration Act priority public uses are hunting, fishing, wildlife observation, photography, and environmental education and interpretation. These uses are encouraged and will receive emphasis in management of public use of the Refuges.

Both consumptive (e.g., hunting, fishing, and trapping) and nonconsumptive (e.g., photography and wildlife viewing,) recreation uses are appropriate. Some recreation uses are incidental to others. Camping and hiking may be related to hunting, fishing, wildlife photography, or other recreation uses.

There is often a fine line between subsistence and recreation use (e.g., berry picking). Subsistence uses are addressed under Subsistence Use Management (section 2.3.12). When it is necessary to restrict the taking of fish and wildlife on a refuge in order to protect the continued viability of such populations, the taking of fish and wildlife for nonwasteful subsistence uses on refuges shall be accorded priority over the taking of fish and wildlife for other purposes, in accordance with Title VIII of ANILCA.

The Refuges will be managed to provide recreation experiences in generally natural wildland settings. Recreation use would be managed consistent with the designated management area category. Moderate Management areas will be managed for greater concentrations of visitors than will be Minimal Management and Wilderness areas. The Refuges will manage all recreation use to avoid crowded conditions and to minimize adverse effects to cultural resources, fish and wildlife, wilderness, and other special values of the refuge. Leave No Trace techniques will be the standard.

The least intrusive means of managing use will be employed. Education will be the primary management tool for recreation management, using brochures, maps, signs, and personal contacts. However, if voluntary methods fail, other actions may be taken. Actions that may be taken to manage recreation include limiting commercial guiding and outfitting; regulating use and access subject to the provisions of Section 1110(a) of ANILCA; and recommending changes in state and/or federal fishing, hunting, and/or trapping regulations. When necessary, recreation opportunities may be seasonally or otherwise restricted to minimize user conflicts and to protect the natural or other values of the refuge.

Any restrictions on public use will follow the public participation and closure procedures at 50 CFR Part 36, 43 CFR Part 36, or other applicable regulations. State management actions available through the Master Memorandum of Understanding (see Appendix B of the Revised Comprehensive Conservation Plan and Environmental Impact Statement) and other state management tools will also be utilized where mutually desirable.

Management plans may be prepared for areas of relatively concentrated use.

2.3.15   Outreach

Outreach is two-way communication between the Refuges and the public to establish mutual understanding, promote public involvement, and influence public attitudes and actions. The Refuges will continue to take advantage of partnership opportunities in providing these services, including working with the Alaska Natural History Association; Alaska Public Lands Information Centers; local, state, and other federal agencies; local schools; tribal governments; Alaska Native organizations; and individuals.

Use of outreach as a management tool is key to the success of many of the management activities outlined in this plan. Two outreach activities—environmental education and interpretation—are included in the six priority public uses identified in the Refuge System Improvement Act. Other activities may be developed for use by the refuge staff in the environmental education step down plan. All outreach activities must be continually evaluated to determine whether they fulfill refuge management goals and objectives. The Refuges will ensure that these services are available to all segments of the public, including those with disabilities and those who speak languages other than English. The Environmental Education Plan was developed in 1991 and is updated annually (see step-down plans).

The Refuges will work with the news media, attend public meetings and workshops, develop Internet home pages, invite the public to the Refuges (open houses), and foster one-on-one communication.

2.3.16   Recreation Facilities

Facilities may be provided to support certain recreation uses. Recreation facilities may be located on refuge lands and at administrative sites. Visitor centers and highly developed environmental education and interpretive sites may be located off refuge lands at administrative sites or other appropriate locations. Recreation facilities may include trails, airstrips, environmental education sites, and signs.

All new buildings (e.g., visitor centers, restrooms, public-use cabins, and visitor-contact buildings) and additions and alterations to existing buildings will comply with current accessibility standards. Other recreation facilities are not currently covered under these standards, although access for the disabled will be considered in the design of new or upgraded facilities. As funds are available, existing buildings will be updated to meet these standards.

The level of development and appearance of facilities will be appropriate for the management category of the area in which they are located. More intensive and sophisticated facilities will be constructed in the Moderate Management category; more rustic and rudimentary facilities will occur in the other management categories.

2.3.16.1   Cabins

Special use permits are required for subsistence and commercial cabins. Management of existing cabins and review of proposals for construction of new cabins for traditional uses will be in accordance with the Service's cabin regulations (50 CFR 36.33). Private recreation use cabins will not be authorized.

Public-use cabins are intended to provide the public with unique opportunities to enjoy and use the Refuges. They also help ensure public health and safety in bad weather and emergencies.

2.3.16.2   Temporary Facilities

Per Section 1316 of ANILCA, the Refuges will allow the use of temporary campsites, tent platforms, shelters, and other temporary facilities and equipment directly and necessarily related to the taking of fish and wildlife, provided these facilities are not detrimental to the purposes of the refuge. Special-use permits may be issued for tent frames, caches, smokehouses, and other facilities. Appropriate stipulations will be included in the special use permits to ensure protection of refuge resources.

The following criteria will be considered in evaluating applications for temporary facilities:

> Where feasible, they will be located in a manner to not displace or compete with existing public uses.

> They will be located away from the vicinity of existing cabins.

> They will be located on sites that are not currently popular campsites.

> They will be located to minimize displacement of wildlife.

> The following conditions may be imposed on temporary-facility special use permits:

> The time of occupancy will coincide with the state and/or federal hunting, fishing, and/or trapping season for the species for which the temporary facility is being used.

> At the end of the specified occupancy, tents and other readily portable materials will be removed.

To the extent feasible, temporary structures will be built with materials that blend into and are compatible with the surrounding landscape.

To the extent feasible, temporary facilities will be screened from water and located so that they are as unobtrusive as possible when viewed from trails and areas of significant public use.

2.3.17   Commercial-Use Management

Commercial uses are activities involving use of a refuge or its resources for a profit. Subsistence uses are not included in commercial uses. Refer to section 2.3.12 for policies related to subsistence.

Except for activities where specific property rights are held by entities other than the federal government (e.g., mining on valid claims under the 1872 Mining Law), or where specifically exempted by law, all commercial uses must comply with both the National Environmental Policy Act (NEPA) and the compatibility requirements of the National Wildlife Refuge System Administration Act. A written authorization (such as a special use permit) is required to conduct commercial activities on a refuge. Compliance with NEPA and a compatibility determination will be required prior to deciding whether to authorize a commercial use. Prior to authorizing any economic use of a natural resource, the refuge manager must determine that each economic use, except for proposed activities authorized by ANILCA, contributes to the achievement of refuge purposes or the National Wildlife Refuge System mission (50 CFR 29.1). See section 2.3.19 for restrictions on commercial activities within designated Wilderness Areas.

2.3.17.1   Mineral Exploration and Development

Oil and Gas Assessment

Geological and geophysical studies, including subsurface core sampling and seismic activities, require special use permits with site-specific stipulations that ensure compatibility with refuge purposes and consistency with the management objectives of this Plan. Other than the rights reserved to the United States under Section 1010(a) of ANILCA, these activities will not be allowed in designated Wilderness.

Oil and Gas Leasing

Oil and gas leasing may be allowed only in Intensive Management areas. These Refuges have no Intensive Management areas; a Plan revision would be necessary to reclassify lands into this category before leasing could occur.

Oil and gas leasing will not be authorized until completion of the following:

An assessment of potential

A national interest determination

A compatibility determination, where applicable

A Comprehensive Conservation Plan amendment

During this process, the Service will seek the views of state and local governments and other interested parties, in accordance with Section 1008(b)(2) of ANILCA.

If leasing is authorized, lease holders will be subject to federal leasing regulations (43 CFR 3100) and appropriate state regulations. Leases will be subject to stipulations on access, seasonal use, and site revegetation; operators would be required to use technology that minimizes impacts on fish, wildlife, and habitat. The Refuge will work closely with leaseholders to minimize adverse effects of mineral exploration and extraction on Refuges resources and recreation opportunities.

Sand, Gravel, and Other Common Variety (Saleable) Minerals

Common variety minerals—such as sand, gravel, stone, limestone, pumice, pumicite, cinders, and clay—may be sold pursuant to the Materials Act of July 31, 1947 (30 U.S.C. 601, 602), as amended. Regulations are found at 43 CFR 3600. Disposal is also authorized under the Refuge Revenue Sharing Act (16 U.S.C. 715s). See Part 612 FW 1 of the Service Manual (USFWS). Extraction may be authorized, where compatible, in Moderate Management areas to support construction and maintenance projects on or near refuge lands if no reasonable material sites exist off refuge lands.

Other Mineral Leasing

In general, mineral leasing is not allowed on refuge land. Geothermal leasing is not allowed on the Refuges under Section 1014(c) of the Geothermal Steam Act (30 U.S.C. 1014). Coal mining is also prohibited, subject to valid existing rights, under Section 16 of the Federal Coal Leasing Amendment Act of 1975 (30 U.S.C. 201 Notes) and the Surface Mining Control and Reclamation Act of 1977 (30 U.S.C. 1272; 43 CFR 3400.2). In specific cases of national need, however, mineral exploration, development, or extraction may be permitted under Section 1502 of ANILCA. The President must determine that the national need for the mineral activity outweighs the other public values of the land. Any recommendation by the President would take effect only after enactment of a joint resolution by Congress.

Alaska Mineral Resource Assessment Program

Section 1010 of ANILCA requires that all federal lands be assessed for their oil, gas, and other mineral potential, although Section 304(c) prohibits new hardrock mining on refuges. Mineral assessment techniques that do not have lasting impacts—such as side-scanning radar, trenching, and core drilling—may be allowed throughout the refuge. Special use permits issued to other government agencies or their contractors for assessment work would include stipulations to ensure that the assessment program is compatible with refuge purposes. For example, stipulations may limit access during nesting, calving, spawning, or other times when fish and wildlife may be especially vulnerable to disturbance.

2.3.17.2 Commercial Recreation Services

Air-taxi and water-taxi operators, wildlife-viewing guides, tour operators, wilderness guides, recreational fishing guides, big-game hunting guides, and others providing recreation services are required, under 50 CFR 27.97, to obtain special use permits to operate on refuge lands. Where the number of special use permits is limited, refuge managers will award permits competitively (see 50 CFR 36.41). Special use permits require compliance with all applicable laws and regulations (e.g., Coast Guard licensing regulations). Permit stipulations ensure that camps; travel methods; storage of food, fish, and game meat; and activities are compatible with refuge purposes and reduce the potential for impacts to resources and to other refuge users. If problems arise relating to commercial recreation activities—such as disturbance of active nests, conflicts with subsistence use, chronic incidence of bears getting into food, or violations of state or federal regulations—the refuges may modify or terminate use under the special use permit stipulations. The Refuges will monitor the number and type of guides and outfitters operating in the refuge and the number of their clients and will, if necessary, further regulate use.

Under Section 1307 of ANILCA, local preference is provided for all new commercial visitor services except guiding for recreational hunting and fishing. Regulations defining local preference are in 50 CFR 36.37.

2.3.17.3 Commercial Fishing and Related Facilities

Under Section 304(d) of ANILCA, the Service will continue to allow individuals with valid commercial fishing rights or privileges to operate on the Refuges. The use of campsites, cabins, motor vehicles, and aircraft on the Refuges in support of commercial fishing is subject to reasonable regulation. Section 304(d) provides for restricting commercial fishing rights if the use is determined to be inconsistent with refuge purposes *and* to be a "significant expansion of commercial fishing activities . . . beyond the level of such activities during 1979." The Service recognizes that fishery levels are cyclic and will take that into consideration when applying the 1979-level criteria. Any new fishery and related facilities and equipment will have to meet the compatibility standard.

Aquaculture, mariculture support facilities, and seafood processing plants will not be allowed.

2.3.17.4 Commercial Harvest of Timber and Firewood

Commercial harvest of timber and firewood will only be authorized under a special use permit and when necessary to fulfill overall refuge management objectives. Within Moderate and Minimal Management categories, commercial harvest of timber and firewood to accomplish management objectives will only occur when an approved refuge fire management plan identifies the need to reduce fuel loads in an area.

Applicable federal and State of Alaska guidelines for timber management will be followed.

2.3.17.5 Commercial Gathering of Other Resources

Gathering of other resources (e.g., antlers and mushrooms) requires a special use permit under 50 CFR 27.51.

2.3.17.6 Commercial Filming and Recording Activities

It is Service policy to provide refuge access and/or assistance to firms and individuals in the pursuit of commercial visual and audio recordings. Such access or assistance will not be provided if visual and audio recordings are incompatible with refuge purposes or the mission of the National Wildlife Refuge System. Commercial films, television production, or sound tracks made within refuges for other than news purposes require a special use permit or authorization (see 43 CFR 5.1).

Commercial filming or recording activities such as videotaping, audio taping, and photography for the purpose of advertising products and services are subject to an A/V Production Permit (see USFWS Refuge Manual 8 RM Section 16).

Permits are not required for still photography on refuge lands open to the general public (P.L. 106-206).

2.3.17.7 Other Commercial Uses

Generally, other commercial uses such as grazing, agriculture, and hydroelectric power development will not be allowed. An exception may be made for low-head or small run-of-the-river hydropower facilities. These may be authorized on a case-by-case basis. See section 2.3.13.6 for transmission lines, pipelines, and other rights-of-way addressed in Title XI of ANILCA.

2.3.18 Environmental Contaminants Identification and Cleanup

One goal of the National Wildlife Refuge System Administration Act is to maintain the biological integrity, diversity, and environmental health of the system. In support of this goal, the Service has studied environmental contaminants that may threaten trust species (i.e., those species for which the Service has primary jurisdiction) and other refuge resources. This work will continue as new concerns are identified and as funding allows.

An assessment of known or suspected contaminants threats within the Refuges was completed in 2004 as part of the national Contaminants Assessment Process. A contaminant assessment report was prepared for the Refuges.

When contaminants are identified on refuge lands, the Service will initiate discussions with the responsible party or parties to remedy the situation. If the Service caused the contamination, funds will be sought to define the extent and type of the contamination and to remedy it. Appropriate environmental regulations—including the Resource Conservation Recovery Act, Comprehensive Environmental Response and Compensation Liability Act, Oil Pollution Act of 1990, and State of Alaska regulations (e.g., 18 AAC 75)—would be followed during remediation work.

All spills of petroleum products and hazardous materials must be reported to the Alaska Department of Environmental Conservation and to the National Response Center. Incidents also need to be reported to the U.S. Fish & Wildlife Service regional spill response coordinator. The Refuges will refer to the U.S. Fish & Wildlife Service Region 7 Spill Response Contingency Plan when responding to spills.

2.3.19 Management of Areas with Special Designations

2.3.19.1 Management of Designated Wilderness

The Becharof Wilderness Area will be managed in accordance with the Wilderness Act of 1964, as modified by provisions of ANILCA; Service guidelines as found in 6 RM 8 of the Refuge System Manual (Part 610 of the Service Manual, when approved); and regional policy. Maintaining wilderness values and resources, preserving the wilderness character of the biological and physical resources, and providing opportunities for research and recreation are the management focuses for designated Wilderness.

A minimum-requirements analysis will be conducted for management activities proposed within the Wilderness Area. This two-step process involves determining if an essential task should be conducted in the Wilderness Area and then determining the combination of methods, equipment, or administrative practices necessary to successfully and safely administer the refuge and accomplish Wilderness management objectives.

Certain activities are legislatively prohibited in designated Wilderness, including oil, gas, and other mineral leasing and most surface-disturbing activities. Other activities—including subsistence use, access for traditional activities, and traditional commercial recreation activities (e.g., guiding and outfitting)—will continue to be allowed where compatible with Wilderness management and refuge and system purposes. Other commercial enterprises—such as fishery-enhancement activities with a primary purpose of enhancing commercial fishing operations—are not allowed.

Generally, motorized and mechanized equipment and transport are prohibited by the Wilderness Act. Several exceptions, however, were identified in ANILCA:

> For access for subsistence purposes (Section 811)

> For access for traditional activities and to and from villages and homesites (Section 1110[a])

> For access to state- or privately owned lands (including subsurface rights), valid mining claims, or other valid occupancy (Section 1110 [b])
>
> For mineral assessment purposes, as part of the Alaska Mineral Resource Assessment Program (Section 1010)

Details of these provisions can be found under the appropriate headings in section 2 of the Revised Comprehensive Conservation Plan and Environmental Impact Statement.

Under 50 CFR 35.5(b), regional policy (RW-16) allows local residents engaged in subsistence activities to use chainsaws. 50 CFR 36.39(c) specifies that off-road vehicles (ORVs) with a maximum weight of 650 pounds may be used for subsistence purposes. Other motorized and mechanized equipment not related to transportation (such as generators and water pumps) are not allowed.

Granting rights-of-way for transportation or utility systems through designated Wilderness requires a Presidential recommendation for Congressional approval (Section 1106[b] of ANILCA) (see section 2.3.13.6).

A step-down Wilderness Stewardship plan will be prepared for the Becharof Wilderness to address in greater detail the resources, uses, and management of the Wilderness Area. Specific details will be included on how the broad management directions provided in the Conservation Plan will be applied to protect the specific wilderness characteristics identified in the Plan. The step-down plan would be prepared in cooperation with the State of Alaska and would include appropriate public involvement.

2.3.19.2 *Mount Veniaminof National Natural Landmark*

Mount Veniaminof was determined to be eligible for Natural Landmark status in 1967. It was so designated by the Secretary of the Interior in August 1970. This unique active volcano is located in the Chignik Unit of the Alaska Peninsula Refuge. Its peak lies about 50 miles east-northeast of Port Moller on Bristol Bay and 40 miles west-southwest of Chignik Bay on the Pacific. It is approximately 450 miles southwest of Anchorage.

Although the National Natural Landmarks Program is administered by the National Park Service, the Mount Veniaminof National Natural Landmark is administered by the Fish & Wildlife Service. Designation recognizes the national significance of the property and encourages its preservation without requiring acquisition. Designation does not dictate use of the property. The Minimal Management category currently applied to the landmark preserves its values. The objective of the program is long-term preservation through voluntary commitment of public and private owners to protect the outstanding values of the area.

2.3.20   Refuge Administration

2.3.20.1   Administrative Sites and Visitor Facilities

Administrative sites include temporary and permanent field camps, residences, offices, and associated storage, communication, and transportation facilities. The type of administrative site and level of development will be consistent with the management intent of the management category in which they are constructed. Administrative field camps or other administrative facilities within Minimal and Wilderness management categories will only be allowed when required to meet management objectives, when no reasonable alternative sites exist and when the facilities are essential to protect the health and safety of employees. New facilities would only be the minimum required to meet long-term needs.

Fuel storage or other hazardous material storage in conjunction with administrative sites will meet all federal and state requirements for spill containment and storage. Hazardous materials stored within the Wilderness Management category lands will be in small (55-gallon or less) containers.

Under Section 1306 of ANILCA, the Secretary of the Interior may establish administrative sites and visitor facilities, either within or outside the boundaries of a conservation system unit, in accordance with the unit's management plan and for the purposes of ensuring the preservation, protection, and proper management of said unit. This section further states that to the "extent practicable and desirable, the Secretary shall attempt to locate such sites and facilities on Native lands in the vicinity of the unit."

Department of Interior guidelines, developed in 1995, implementing Section 1306 of ANILCA require that prior to initiating a search for an administrative site or visitor facility, site-selection criteria be developed, with public input, and all proposals be evaluated according to the site-selection criteria. If it is determined that Native lands satisfy the site-selection criteria and are desirable and practicable for the intended use, the highest-ranking Native lands shall be selected as the preferred site, subject to a specific site evaluation. If no Native lands satisfy the site-selection criteria, the highest-ranking parcel will become the preferred site. Public comments will be considered prior to making a final decision.

Applicability of Refuge Regulations to Off-Refuge Administrative and Visitor Facility Sites

Part 50 of CFR 36.1(c) authorizes the Service to enforce regulations concerning public safety and protection of government property, as well as State of Alaska fish and wildlife regulations, on administrative and visitor facility sites that may be held in fee or less-than-fee title and are either inside or outside the approved boundaries of any Alaska national wildlife refuge.

2.3.20.2   Step Down Plans

Some management programs are addressed in sufficient detail in the Revised Comprehensive Conservation Plan and Environmental Impact Statement to be integrated directly into the budgetary process. For other programs, it may be necessary to prepare step-down management plans to implement general strategies identified in the conservation plan. Additional information on the step-down planning process can be found in Part 602, FW 3, of the Service Manual (USFWS) and section 5.1 of this plan.

The following step-down management plans are required for these Refuges:

> Cultural Resources Guide - Completed in 1996, to be revised in 2008
>
> Environmental Education Plan - Completed in 1991, reviewed annually
>
> Facilities Management - Completed in 1997, to be revised in 2007
>
> Fisheries Management - Updated in 1994, to be revised in 2008
>
> Habitat Inventory - To be completed by 2007
>
> Land Protection - Completed in 2002
>
> Public Use Management - Completed in 1994, revised in this Conservation Plan
>
> Station Safety Plan - Reviewed annually
>
> Water Resources - To be completed by 2010
>
> Wildlife Inventory - To be completed by 2007
>
> Wilderness Stewardship - To be completed by 2010

2.3.21   Management Categories

Three management categories—Moderate Management, Minimal Management, and Wilderness—are used to describe management levels on these refuges. A management category is used to define the level of human activity appropriate to a specific area of the refuge. It is a set of refuge management directions applied to an area, in light of its resources and existing and potential uses, to facilitate management and the accomplishment of refuge purposes and goals. Figure 6: Current Management Categories depicts the management categories as they apply to the Refuges.

Table 2: Activities, Uses, and Facilities by Management Category shows those management activities, public uses, commercial uses, and facilities that may be allowed in each management category and under what conditions.

Activities or uses not generally allowed within a management category would require consideration of a plan amendment to change the management category to one which would allow the use prior to approval.

Table 1: Acreages

Management Category	Acreage	Percentage of Refuges
Moderate Management	4,000	0.1
Minimal Management	3,733,400	88.1
Wilderness Management	502,900	11.9
Total Service Administered	4,240,300	100

2.3.21.1 Moderate Management

Moderate Management is meant to allow compatible management actions, public uses, commercial uses, and facilities that may result in changes to the natural environment that are temporary, or permanent, but small in scale and that do not disrupt natural processes. The natural landscape is the dominant feature of Moderate Management areas, although signs of human actions may be visible.

Management actions in the category of Moderate Management will focus on maintaining, restoring, or enhancing habitats to maintain healthy populations of plants and animals where natural processes take over. In general, management facilities, both temporary and permanent, will be allowed for the purposes of gathering data needed to understand and manage resources and natural systems of the Refuges. Structures will be designed to minimize overall visual impact.

Public facilities provided in Moderate Management will, while protecting habitats and resources, allow the public to enjoy and use refuge resources in low numbers over a large area or they will encourage the short-term enjoyment of the Refuges in focused areas. The emphasis is on small facilities that encourage outdoor experiences. Facilities such as public use cabins, rustic campgrounds, kiosks, viewing platforms, trails, and toilets may be provided. Facilities will be designed to blend with the surrounding environment. The Refuges have one Moderate Management area in which ORV use is allowed for recreation purposes (i.e., Yantarni Bay).

Compatible economic activities may be allowed where impacts to natural processes and habitats are temporary (e.g., facilities in support of guiding and outfitting services such as tent platforms or cabins that encourage enhanced public use). All economic activities and facilities require authorizations such as special use permits.

2.3.21.2 *Minimal Management*

Minimal Management is designed to maintain the natural environment with very little evidence of human-caused change. Habitats should be allowed to change and function through natural processes. Administration will ensure that the resource values and environmental characteristics identified in the conservation plan are conserved. Management actions that change existing habitats should be designed and implemented so that a natural appearance is maintained. Public uses, economic activities, and facilities should minimize disturbance to habitats and resources. Ground-disturbing activities are to be avoided whenever possible.

Management actions in this category focus on understanding natural systems and monitoring the health of refuge resources. Generally, no permanent structures are allowed (except cabins). Temporary structures may be allowed in situations in which removal is planned after the period of authorized use and the site can be rehabilitated using plants native to the immediate area. Existing cabins may be allowed for administrative, public-use, subsistence, or commercial or economic (e.g., guiding) purposes. New subsistence or commercial cabins may be authorized if no reasonable alternative sites exist. Public-use or administrative cabins may be constructed if necessary for health and safety.

Public use of the Refuges for wildlife-dependent recreation and subsistence activities is encouraged. Public-use facilities are not generally provided. Mechanized and motorized equipment may be allowed when the overall impacts are temporary or where its use furthers management goals.

Compatible economic activities may be allowed where the evidence of those activities does not last past the season of use, except as noted in the preceding discussion of cabins. The primary economic activities are likely to be guiding and outfitting of recreation activities such as hunting, fishing, hiking, river floating, and sightseeing. All economic activities and facilities require authorizations such as special use permits.

2.3.21.3 *Wilderness*

This management category applies only to the Becharof Wilderness Area, designated by Congress as a unit of the National Wilderness Preservation System. Areas proposed for Wilderness designation will be managed under minimal management, consistent with ANILCA Section 1317(c) and with Service policy. Designated Wilderness will be managed under the Wilderness Act of 1964 and the exceptions provided by ANILCA. Because Wilderness units are part of a nationwide, multi-agency system, the Service recognizes that responsibilities for managing refuge Wilderness go beyond the mission of the Service and that the purposes of the Wilderness Act are within and supplemental to the other purposes for which individual refuges were established.

The history and intent behind the Wilderness Act make Wilderness more than just another category of land management. Wilderness encourages having a broadened perspective of the refuge landscape, one that extends beyond managing it solely as wildlife habitat. Wilderness is managed as an area "retaining its primeval character and influence." In addition, Wilderness provides human visitors with opportunities for solitude and primitive recreation, which may be characterized in terms of experiential dimensions such as discovery, self-reliance, and challenge.

Wilderness Areas are managed to preserve their experiential values as well as aesthetic, scientific, and other related values. Research has shown that some values of Wilderness extend beyond their boundaries to people who may never visit but who benefit from the protection of natural ecological processes—benefits such as clean air and water and the simple knowledge that such places exist. In managing Wilderness, managers are encouraged to consider in decision-making these off-site and symbolic values as well as tangible resource values.

Permanent structures are generally prohibited; excepted are historic and cultural resources and, in certain circumstances, administrative structures or cabins that predate ANILCA, cabins that are necessary for trapping, and public-use cabins necessary for the protection of human health and safety. Facilities and structures are rustic and unobtrusive in appearance.

Compatible commercial uses of Wilderness Areas are generally limited to those activities that facilitate enjoyment of the areas (e.g., guided fishing, hunting, and wilderness trips). All commercial activities and facilities require authorizations (e.g., special use permits).

A variety of management actions may be taken to maintain the wilderness values of the area. Actions such as prescribed fires or invasive-species control may be conducted when it is necessary to protect life or property or when it is necessary to restore, maintain, or protect wilderness values.

2.3.21.4 *Special Management*

Although there are none on these Refuges, Special Management lands are managed within one of the categories described previously but have additional requirements because of their status. An example of Special Management areas would be Research Natural Areas.

Management of Selected Lands

The Service retains management responsibility for lands selected but not yet conveyed to Native village and regional corporations or to the State of Alaska. The appropriate Native corporation or agency of the State of Alaska will be contacted and its views considered prior to implementing a management program or issuing a permit involving these lands. Fees collected for special use or right-of-way permits will be held in escrow until the selected lands are conveyed or relinquished. Management directions for these lands will be the same as for adjacent refuge lands.

2.3.21.5 Management Categories Table

Explanatory Notes

The descriptions of the management categories reflect a clear distinction in the level of action, type of action, and constraints that may be placed on activities or development within the management categories. They should be used to reflect the desired future condition of the area when site-specific proposals are being evaluated. Activities allowed or authorized will be managed differently depending on the management category in which they occur.

Key for Management Categories Table

The following terms are used:

NEPA analysis—All activities, uses, and facilities proposed for a refuge that have the potential to result in significant effects on the environment require an analysis of potential environmental impacts under the National Environmental Policy Act. This analysis may be documented as a categorical exclusion (CE), an environmental assessment (EA), or an environmental impact statement (EIS), depending on the nature of the proposed project.

Compatibility—All activities, uses, and facilities allowed on a refuge, except management actions undertaken by or for the Service, must be compatible with the purposes of the refuge and the mission of the National Wildlife Refuge System. The analysis that occurs results in a compatibility determination. Management activities undertaken by the Service or by volunteers, cooperators, or contractors working for the Service, with limited exception, are exempt from compatibility review (Part 603, Compatibility, of the Service Manual).

Regulations—All activities, uses, and facilities allowed on a refuge must comply with any applicable regulations, as published in the Code of Federal Regulations (CFR). Regulations are developed by the Service through a public process to implement the legal authorities under which the Service manages the National Wildlife Refuge System. For more information on these regulations, see the appropriate topic in Management Directions, section 2.3 of this chapter. For some activities, other federal agency and/or state regulations may also apply.

Temporary—A continuous period of time not to exceed 12 months, except as specifically provided otherwise. Special use permits or other authorizations may prescribe a longer period of time, but the structures or other human-made improvements need to be readily and completely dismantled and removed from the site when the period of authorized use terminates.

The following are definitions for terms used in the table.

Allowed—Activity, use, or facility is allowed under existing NEPA analysis, compatibility determinations, and applicable laws and regulations of the Service, other federal agencies and the State of Alaska.

May be allowed—Activity, use or facility may be allowed subject to site-specific NEPA analysis (including CEs, EAs, and EISs), a specific compatibility determination, and compliance with all applicable laws and regulations of the Service, other federal agencies, and the State of Alaska.

May be authorized—Activity, use, or facility **may be allowed**; a special use permit or other authorization is required.

Not allowed—Activity, use, or facility is not allowed.

The following guidelines apply to all activities, uses, and facilities allowed on a refuge:

Area or time restrictions—All activities and uses allowed on a refuge may be restricted in certain areas or at certain times, at the discretion of the refuge manager and with the appropriate level of public involvement, by emergency (short-term) or permanent regulation, if necessary to protect refuge resources or human health and safety.

Management emergencies—Activities, uses, and facilities not allowed on a refuge or in specific management categories may be allowed if naturally occurring or human-caused actions adversely affect refuge resources or threaten human health and safety.

Table 2: Activities, Uses, and Facilities by Management Category

(Shaded rows describe activities that currently do not occur on the refuges covered by this plan.)

ACTIVITY	MODERATE MANAGEMENT	MINIMAL MANAGEMENT	MANAGEMENT of WILDERNESS
ECOSYSTEM, HABITAT, AND FISH AND WILDLIFE MANAGEMENT			
Ecosystem and Landscape Management			
Collecting Information on and Monitoring Ecosystem Components Data gathering, monitoring, and maintaining a comprehensive database of selected ecosystem components (plants, animals, fish, water, air).	Allowed; see sections 2.3.11.1 and 2.3.11.2	Same as Moderate Management	Same as Moderate Management; see also section 2.3.19.1
Research and Management Access and collection of data necessary for management decisions or to further science.	Service—Allowed ADF&G—Coordinate with refuge manager; see sections 2.3.8.1 and 2.3.11 Other researchers—May be allowed	Same as Moderate Management	Same as Moderate Management; see also section 2.3.19.1
Research and Management Facilities May be permanent or temporary structures or camps, including weirs, counting towers, and sonar counters.	May be allowed; see sections 2.3.10.1 and 2.3.20.1	Same as Moderate Management	Same as Moderate Management; must be consistent with sections 2.3.21.3 and 2.3.19.1
Fish and Wildlife Habitat Management			
Describing, Locating, and Mapping Habitats Development of quantitative, written, and graphic descriptions of fish and wildlife habitat, including water, food, and shelter components.	Allowed; see section 2.3.11.1	Same as Moderate Management	Same as Moderate Management; see also section 2.3.19.1
Habitat Management *Mechanical Treatment* Activities such as cutting, crushing, or mowing of vegetation; water control structures; fencing; artificial nest structures.	May be allowed; see section 2.3.10.1	Not allowed; with exceptions consistent with section 2.3.21.2	Same as Minimal Management; see also section 2.3.19.1

ACTIVITY	MODERATE MANAGEMENT	MINIMAL MANAGEMENT	MANAGEMENT of WILDERNESS
Chemical Treatment Use of chemicals to remove or control nonnative species.	May be allowed; see sections 2.3.10.1 and 2.3.10.3	Same as Moderate Management	Same as Moderate Management; see also section 2.3.19.1
Manual Treatment Use of hand tools to remove, reduce, or modify hazardous plant fuels, or exotic plant species or to modify habitats (e.g., remove beaver dams).	Allowed; see section 2.3.10.1	Same as Moderate Management	Same as Moderate Management; see also section 2.3.19.1
Aquatic Habitat Modifications Activities such as streambank restoration, passage structures, fish barriers, or removal of obstacles that result in physical modification of aquatic habitats to maintain or restore native fish species.	May be allowed; see sections 2.3.10.1 and 2.3.11.10	Same as Moderate Management	Same as Moderate Management; must be consistent with constraints in section 2.3.21.3; see also section 2.3.19.1
Fire Management—Prescribed Fires Fire ignited by management actions to meet specific management objectives.	May be allowed; subject to section 2.3.10.2	Same as Moderate Management consistent with constraints in section 2.3.21.2	Same as Moderate Management; consistent with constraints in sections 2.3.21.3 and 2.3.19.1
Fire Management—Wildland Fire Use The planned use of naturally occurring fires to meet management objectives.	May be allowed; subject to section 2.3.10.2	Same as Moderate Management; limited to constraints in section 2.3.21.2	Same as Moderate Management; limited to constraints in sections 2.3.21.3 and 2.3.19.1
Fire Management—Fire Suppression Management actions intended to protect identified resources from a fire, extinguish a fire, or alter a fire's direction of spread	Allowed; subject to section 2.3.10.2	Same as Moderate Management; see also section 2.3.21.2	Same as Moderate Management; see also sections 2.3.21.3 and 2.3.19.1
Weed Control Monitoring, extirpation, control, removal and/or relocation and other management practices for pest and nonnative plant species.	May be allowed; see section 2.3.10.3	Same as Moderate Management	Same as Moderate Management; see also section 2.3.19.1

ACTIVITY	MODERATE MANAGEMENT	MINIMAL MANAGEMENT	MANAGEMENT of WILDERNESS
Water Quality and Quantity Management Monitoring of water quality and quantity to identify baseline data and for management purposes; includes installation of gauging stations.	Allowed; see section 2.3.9.2	Same as Moderate Management	Same as Moderate Management; see also section 2.3.19.1
Fish and Wildlife Population Management			
Reintroduction of Species The reintroduction of native species to restore natural diversity of fish, wildlife, and habitats.	May be allowed; see section 2.3.11.6	Same as Moderate Management	Same as Moderate Management; see also section 2.3.19.1
Fish and Wildlife Control The control, relocation, sterilization, removal, or other management of native species, including predators, to maintain natural diversity of fish, wildlife, and habitats; favor other fish or wildlife populations; protect reintroduced, threatened, or endangered species; or to restore depleted native populations.	May be allowed; see section 2.3.11.6	Same as Moderate Management	Same as Moderate Management; see also section 2.3.19.1
Nonnative Species Management The removal or control of nonnative species (including predators).	May be allowed; see section 2.3.11.8	Same as Moderate Management; use least-intrusive methods	Same as Minimal Management; see also section 2.3.19.1
Pest Management and Disease Prevention and Control Relocation or removal of organisms that threaten human health or survival of native fish, wildlife, or plant species. Management practices directed at controlling pathogens that threaten fish, wildlife, and people such as rabies and parasite control.	May be allowed; see section 2.3.11.9	Same as Moderate Management	Same as Moderate Management; see also section 2.3.19.1
Fishery Restoration Actions taken to restore fish access to spawning and rearing habitat or actions taken to restore populations to historic levels. Includes harvest management, escapement goals, habitat restoration, stocking, egg incubation boxes, and lake fertilization.	May be allowed; see section 2.3.11.10	Same as Moderate Management	Same as Moderate Management; see also section 2.3.19.1

ACTIVITY	MODERATE MANAGEMENT	MINIMAL MANAGEMENT	MANAGEMENT of WILDERNESS
Fishery Restoration Facilities Fisheries facilities may be permanent or temporary and may include hatcheries, fish ladders, fish passages, fish barriers, and associated structures.	May be authorized; see sections 2.3.11.10 and 2.3.20.1	Same as Moderate Management; see also section 2.3.21.2	Same as Moderate Management; see also sections 2.3.21.3 and 2.3.19.1
Fishery Enhancement Activities applied to a fish stock to supplement numbers of harvestable fish to a level beyond what could be naturally produced based upon a determination or reasonable estimate of historic levels.	May be allowed; see section 2.3.11.11	Same as Moderate Management	Same as Moderate Management; see also section 2.3.19.1
Fishery Enhancement Facilities May be permanent or temporary and may include hatcheries, egg incubation boxes, fish ladders, fish passages, fish barriers, and associated structures.	May be authorized, see sections 2.3.11.11 and 2.3.20.1	Same as Moderate Management; see also section 2.3.21.2	Same as Moderate Management; see also sections 2.3.21.3 and 2.3.19.1
Native Fish Introductions Movement of native fish species within a drainage on the refuge to areas where they have not historically existed.	May be allowed; see section 2.3.11.6	Not allowed	Same as Minimal Management
Nonnative Species Introductions Introduction of species not naturally occurring within a watershed.	Not allowed; see section 2.3.11.6	Same as Moderate Management	Same as Moderate Management
SUBSISTENCE			
Fishing, Hunting, Trapping, and Berry Picking The taking of fish and wildlife and other natural resources for personal consumption, as provided by law.	Allowed; see section 2.3.12	Same as Moderate Management	Same as Moderate Management
Collection of House Logs and Firewood Harvesting live standing timber greater than 6 inches diameter at breast height for personal or extended family use.	May be authorized; see section 2.3.12	Same as Moderate Management	Same as Moderate Management
Collection of House Logs and Firewood Live trees less than 3 inched diameter at breast height and dead standing or down timber for personal or extended family use.	Allowed; see section 2.3.12	Same as Moderate Management	Same as Moderate Management
Collection of House Logs and Firewood Live trees between 3 and 6 inches diameter at breast height for personal or extended family use.	May be authorized; see section 2.3.12	Same as Moderate Management	Same as Moderate Management

ACTIVITY	MODERATE MANAGEMENT	MINIMAL MANAGEMENT	MANAGEMENT of WILDERNESS
Collection of Other Plant Materials Harvesting trees less than 6 inches diameter at breast height for trapping and other purposes; harvesting grass, bark, other plant materials used as food, in making handicrafts, or for other subsistence purposes.	Allowed; see section 2.3.12	Same as Moderate Management	Same as Moderate Management
Access Use of snowmachines, motorboats, and other means of surface transportation traditionally employed for subsistence purposes.	Allowed; see section 2.3.12.1	Same as Moderate Management	Same as Moderate Management
Temporary Facilities Establishment and use of tent platforms, shelters, and other temporary facilities and equipment directly related to the taking of fish and wildlife.	Allowed; see section 2.3.16.2	Same as Moderate Management	Same as Moderate Management
Subsistence Cabins	See CABINS and section 2.3.16.1		

ACCESS
(restrictions subject to provisions of Section 1110 of ANILCA; access for subsistence purposes discussed in SUBSISTENCE section)

Nonmotorized

	MODERATE MANAGEMENT	MINIMAL MANAGEMENT	MANAGEMENT of WILDERNESS
Foot	Allowed; see sections 2.3.13.1 and 2.3.14	Same as Moderate Management	Same as Moderate Management
Dogs and Dog Teams	Allowed; see sections 2.3.13.1 and 2.3.14	Same as Moderate Management	Same as Moderate Management
Other Domestic Animals Includes horses, mules, llamas, and other domestic animals.	Allowed, see sections 2.3.13.1 and 2.3.14	Same as Moderate Management	Same as Moderate Management
Bicycles Includes all types of bicycles (e.g., road, BMX, mountain)	Allowed; see sections 2.3.13.1 and 2.3.14	Same as Moderate Management	Same as Moderate Management
Nonmotorized Boats Includes canoes, kayaks, rafts, etc.	Allowed; see sections 2.3.13.1 and 2.3.14	Same as Moderate Management	Same as Moderate Management

Motorized

ACTIVITY	MODERATE MANAGEMENT	MINIMAL MANAGEMENT	MANAGEMENT of WILDERNESS
Motorboats Includes inboard and outboard motor power boats, including jet boats; does not include jet-driven personal watercraft, air boats, and air-cushion vehicles.	Allowed; see sections 2.3.13.1 and 2.3.14	Same as Moderate Management	Same as Moderate Management
Highway Vehicles	May be allowed on designated roads.	Not allowed	Same as Minimal Management
Off-Road Vehicles (All-Terrain Vehicles) Excludes air boats and air-cushion vehicles	Allowed see section 2.3.13.2	Not allowed; see also section 2.3.12.1	Same as Minimal Management
Airplanes Fixed-wing aircraft such as float planes and wheeled planes	Allowed; see sections 2.3.13.1 and 2.3.14	Same as Moderate Management	Same as Moderate Management
Helicopters Includes all rotary-wing aircraft	May be authorized; see section 2.3.13.2	Same as Moderate Management	Same as Moderate Management; must be consistent with sections 2.3.21.3 and 2.3.19.1
Snowmachines (Snowmobiles) A self-propelled vehicle intended for off-road travel primarily on snow having a curb weight of not more than 1,000 pounds (450 kg), driven by track or tracks in contact with the snow.	Allowed; see sections 2.3.13.1 and 2.3.14	Same as Moderate Management	Same as Moderate Management
PUBLIC USE, RECREATION, and OUTREACH ACTIVITIES *(Also see ACCESS section)*			
Hunting*, Fishing*, Trapping, Walking, Hiking, Camping at Undeveloped Sites, Wildlife Observation*, and Dog Sledding Note: * = priority public use	Allowed; see sections 2.3.1 and 2.3.14	Same as Moderate Management	Same as Moderate Management
Wildlife Photography* and General Photography—Also see COMMERCIAL USES Note: * = priority public use	Allowed; see sections 2.3.1 and 2.3.14	Same as Moderate Management	Same as Moderate Management
Boating and Snowmachining Motorized and nonmotorized boating (excluding air boats and air-cushion vehicles) and snowmachining. Also see ACCESS.	Allowed; see sections 2.3.1, 2.3.14, and 2.3.13.1	Same as Moderate Management	Same as Moderate Management

ACTIVITY	MODERATE MANAGEMENT	MINIMAL MANAGEMENT	MANAGEMENT of WILDERNESS
Interpretation*, Environmental Education*, and other Outreach Activities Note: * = priority public use	Allowed; see sections 2.3.21.1 and 2.3.15	Same as Moderate Management; see sections 2.3.21.2 and 2.3.15	Same as Moderate Management; see sections 2.3.21.3 and 2.3.15
PUBLIC USE and RECREATION FACILITIES			
Recreation Facilities Facilities provided by the Service	May be allowed; see sections 2.3.21.1 and 2.3.16	Same as Moderate Management see sections 2.3.21.2 and 2.3.16	Same as Moderate Management; see sections 2.3.21.3, 2.3.16, and 2.3.19
All-Weather Roads and associated developments, including bridges.	May be allowed; see section 2.3.21.1	Not allowed	Same as Minimal Management
Unimproved Roads	Allowed; see section 2.3.16	Not allowed	Same as Minimal Management
Off-Road Vehicle (All-Terrain Vehicle) Trails and Routes	May be allowed; see section 2.3.16	Not allowed	Same as Minimal Management
Roadside Exhibits and Waysides	May be allowed; see section 2.3.16	Not applicable	Not applicable
Constructed and Maintained Airstrips	May be allowed; see section 2.3.16	Not allowed	Same as Minimal Management
Cleared Landing Strips and Areas	May be allowed; see section 2.3.16	Same as Moderate Management	Not allowed; see also section 2.3.19.1
Constructed Hiking Trails Includes bridges, boardwalks, trailheads, and related facilities	May be allowed; see sections 2.3.21.1 and 2.3.16	Same as Moderate Management; see sections 2.3.21.2 and 2.3.16	Same as Moderate Management; see sections 2.3.21.3, 2.3.16, and 2.3.19
Designated Hiking Routes Unimproved and unmaintained trails; may be designated by signs, cairns, and/or on maps.	Allowed; see sections 2.3.21.1 and 2.3.16	Same as Moderate Management; consistent with sections 2.3.21.2 and 2.3.16	Same as Moderate Management; consistent with sections 2.3.21.3, 2.3.16, and 2.3.19

ACTIVITY	MODERATE MANAGEMENT	MINIMAL MANAGEMENT	MANAGEMENT of WILDERNESS
Boat Launches and Docks Designated sites for launching and storing watercraft.	May be allowed; see sections 2.3.21.1 and 2.3.16	Same as Moderate Management see section 2.3.21.2	Same as Moderate Management; see sections 2.3.21.3 and 2.3.19.1
Visitor Contact Facilities A variety of staffed and unstaffed facilities providing information on the refuge and its resources to the public; facilities range from visitor centers to kiosks and signs.	May be allowed; see section 2.3.16 consistent with direction in section 2.3.21.1	Same as Moderate Management consistent with direction in section 2.3.21.2	Generally not allowed except as provided in section 2.3.19.1; see also section 2.3.21.3
Hardened Campsites Areas where people can camp that are accessible by vehicle or on foot but where the only facilities provided are for public health and safety and/or resource protection; may include gravel pads for tents, hardened trails, and/or primitive toilets.	Allowed; see also section 2.3.21.1	Same as Moderate Management; see also section 2.3.21.2	Same as Moderate Management when consistent with sections 2.3.21.3 and 2.3.19.1
Temporary Facilities Includes tent frames, caches, and other similar or related facilities; does not include cabins. See also SUBSISTENCE, ADMINISTRATIVE FACILITIES, and COMMERCIAL USES.	Allowed; see section 2.3.16.2	Same as Moderate Management	Same as Moderate Management
CABINS *(and other related structures such as outdoor toilets, and fish-drying racks)*			
Public Use Cabin A cabin administered by the Service and available for use by the public; intended only for short-term public recreation use and occupancy.	Existing cabins allowed to remain; new cabins may be allowed; see section 2.3.16.1	Same as Moderate Management consistent with section 2.3.21.2	Same as Moderate Management, consistent with sections 2.3.21.3 and 2.3.19.1
Administrative Cabin Any cabin primarily used by refuge staff or other authorized personnel for the administration of the refuge.	May be allowed; see section 2.3.20.1	Same as Moderate Management, consistent with section 2.3.21.2	Same as Moderate Management, consistent with sections 2.3.21.3 and 2.3.19.1
Subsistence Cabin Any cabin necessary for health and safety and to provide for the continuation of ongoing subsistence activities; **not** for recreation use.	Existing cabins allowed; new cabins may be authorized; see section 2.3.16.1	Same as Moderate Management	Same as Moderate Management

ACTIVITY	MODERATE MANAGEMENT	MINIMAL MANAGEMENT	MANAGEMENT of WILDERNESS
Commercial Cabin Any cabin that is used in association with a commercial operation, including commercial fishing activities and recreational guiding services.	Existing cabins allowed to remain, new cabins may be authorized; see section 2.3.16.1	Same as Moderate Management	Existing cabins (pre-designation)—same as Moderate Management; new cabins not allowed.
Other Cabins Cabins associated with authorized uses by other government agencies.	May be allowed	May be allowed, consistent with section 2.3.21.2	Same as Moderate Management, consistent with sections 2.3.21.3 and 2.3.19.1
ADMINISTRATIVE FACILITIES			
Administrative Field Camps *Temporary* facilities used by refuge staff and other authorized personnel to support individual (generally) field projects; may include tent frames and temporary/portable outhouses, shower facilities, storage/maintenance facilities, and caches.	May be allowed; see section 2.3.20.1	Same as Moderate Management	Same as Moderate Management; consistent with sections 2.3.21.3 and 2.3.19.1
Administrative Field Sites *Permanent* facilities used by refuge staff or other authorized personnel for the administration of the refuge. Includes administrative cabins and related structures (see CABINS above) and larger multi-facility administrative sites necessary to support ongoing field projects, research, and other management activities. Temporary facilities, to meet short-term needs, may supplement the permanent facilities at these sites.	Use of existing sites allowed, including replacement of existing facilities as necessary; new sites may be allowed; see section 2.3.20.1	Same as Moderate Management	Same as Moderate Management; see also section 2.3.19.1
Refuge Administrative Office Complex Facilities necessary to house refuge operations, outreach, and maintenance activities and associated infrastructure; includes staff offices, storage, maintenance, and other facilities, parking lots, and so forth.	Not allowed	Same as Moderate Management	Same as Moderate Management

ACTIVITY	MODERATE MANAGEMENT	MINIMAL MANAGEMENT	MANAGEMENT of WILDERNESS
Hazardous Materials Storage Sites including appropriate structures and equipment necessary for the storage and transfer of fuels and other hazardous materials used for administrative purposes; must be in compliance with all federal and state requirements.	May be allowed; see section 2.3.20.1	Same as Moderate Management	Same as Moderate Management; see also sections 2.3.21.3 and 2.3.19.1
Residences Residential housing for refuge staff and their families; includes single- and multi-family dwellings.	Not allowed	Same as Moderate Management	Same as Moderate Management
Bunkhouses Quarters to house temporary and similar employees, volunteers, visitors, and other agency personnel.	May be allowed; see section 2.3.20.1	Not allowed	Same as Minimal Management
Boat Launching Sites and Docks	See PUBLIC-USE FACILITIES		
Float-Plane Bases Improved sites for docking and storage of float-equipped aircraft	May be allowed; see section 2.3.20.1	Not allowed	Same as Minimal Management
Aircraft Hangars Facilities for storage of aircraft	Not allowed	Same as Moderate Management	Same as Moderate Management
Radio Repeater Sites Sites used to maintain radio communications equipment; may include helispots for access.	May be allowed; see section 2.3.20.1	Same as Moderate Management	Same as Moderate Management; consistent with sections 2.3.21.3 and 2.3.19.1

COMMERCIAL USES

(Does not include subsistence use; see SUBSISTENCE section of this table. Except as specifically noted, a written authorization in the form of a special use permit or other document is required for economic use of a refuge.)

MINERAL EXPLORATION

	MODERATE MANAGEMENT	MINIMAL MANAGEMENT	MANAGEMENT of WILDERNESS
Surface Geological Studies Includes surface rock collecting and geological mapping activities (includes helicopter or fixed-wing access).	May be authorized; see section 2.3.17.1	Same as Moderate Management	Same as Moderate Management

ACTIVITY	MODERATE MANAGEMENT	MINIMAL MANAGEMENT	MANAGEMENT of WILDERNESS
Geophysical Exploration and Seismic **Studies** Examination of subsurface rock formations through devices that set off and record vibrations in the earth. Usually involves mechanized surface transportation, but may be helicopter supported; includes studies conducted for the Department of the Interior.	May be authorized; see section 2.3.17.1	Same as Moderate Management	Not allowed except as discussed in section 2.3.17.1
Core Sampling Using helicopter-transported motorized drill rig to extract subsurface rock samples; does not include exploratory wells; includes sampling conducted for Department of the Interior.	May be authorized; see section 2.3.17.1	Same as Moderate Management	Not allowed except as discussed in section 2.3.17.1
Other Geophysical Studies Helicopter-supported gravity and magnetic surveys and other minimal-impact activities that do not require mechanized surface transportation.	May be authorized; see section 2.3.17.1	Same as Moderate Management	Not allowed except as discussed in section 2.3.17.1
Oil and Gas Leasing Leasing, drilling, and extraction of oil and gas for commercial purposes. Includes all associated above- and below-ground facilities.	Not allowed; see section 2.3.17.1	Same as Moderate Management	Same as Moderate Management
Sale of Sand, Gravel, and Other Common Variety Minerals Extraction of sand, gravel, and other saleable minerals for commercial purposes; includes noncommercial use by federal, state, and local agencies.	May be authorized; see section 2.3.17.1	Not allowed	Same as Minimal Management
Other Mineral Leasing Includes the extraction of coal, geothermal resources, potassium, sodium, phosphate, sulfur, or other leaseable minerals for commercial purposes.	Not allowed; see section 2.3.17.1	Same as Moderate Management	Same as Moderate Management
Mining of Hardrock Minerals Development of valid (pre-ANILCA) mining claims (lode, placer, and mill sites) on refuge lands for the purpose of extracting hardrock minerals.	Not allowed	Same as Moderate Management	Same as Moderate Management
COMMERCIAL RECREATION *(Includes all forms of guiding, including those operated by nonprofit, educational, and other noncommercial groups)*			
Guiding and Outfitting	May be authorized; see section 2.3.17.2	Same as Moderate Management	Same as Moderate Management

ACTIVITY	MODERATE MANAGEMENT	MINIMAL MANAGEMENT	MANAGEMENT of WILDERNESS
Transporting	May be authorized; see section 2.3.17.2	Same as Moderate Management	Same as Moderate Management
Fixed-Wing Air Taxis	May be authorized; see section 2.3.17.2	Same as Moderate Management	Same as Moderate Management
Helicopter Air Taxis	May be authorized; see section 2.3.17.2	Same as Moderate Management	Not allowed except as discussed in section 2.3.13.2
Bus and Auto Tours	May be authorized; see section 2.3.17.2	Not applicable	Not applicable
Other Commercial Activities			
Commercial Filming, Videotaping, and Audiotaping	May be authorized; see section 2.3.17.6	Same as Moderate Management	Same as Moderate Management
Grazing	Not allowed; see sections 2.3.17 and 2.3.17.7	Same as Moderate Management	Same as Moderate Management
Agriculture (Commercial)	Not allowed; see sections 2.3.17 and 2.3.17.7	Same as Moderate Management	Same as Moderate Management
Commercial Fishery Support Facilities At or below 1979 levels	Allowed; see section 2.3.17.3	Same as Moderate Management	Same as Moderate Management
Commercial Fishery Support Facilities Above 1979 levels	May be authorized; see section 2.3.17.3	Same as Moderate Management	Not allowed
Seafood Processing	Not allowed; see section 2.3.17.3	Same as Moderate Management	Same as Moderate Management
Aquaculture and Mariculture Support Facilities	Not allowed	Same as Moderate Management	Same as Moderate Management

ACTIVITY	MODERATE MANAGEMENT	MINIMAL MANAGEMENT	MANAGEMENT of WILDERNESS
Commercial Timber and Firewood Harvest	May be authorized; see section 2.3.17.4	Same as Moderate Management	Not allowed
Commercial Gathering of Other Refuge Resources	May be authorized; see section 2.3.17.5	Not allowed	Same as Minimal Management
Transportation and Utility Systems Includes transmission lines, pipelines, telephone and electrical power lines, oil and gas pipelines, communication systems, roads, airstrips, and other necessary related facilities. Does not include facilities associated with on-refuge oil and gas development.	May be authorized; see section 2.3.13.6	Not allowed: See 2.3.13.6	Same as Minimal Management
Navigation Aids and Other Facilities Includes air and water navigation aids and related facilities, communication sites and related facilities, facilities for national defense purposes and related air/water navigation aids, and facilities for weather, climate, and fisheries research and monitoring; includes both private and government facilities.	Existing and new facilities allowed; see section 2.3.13.10	Same as Moderate Management	Same as Moderate Management; see also section 2.3.21.3
Major Hydroelectric Power Development Hydroelectric dams creating a change in streamflow with an elevation change and reservoir behind the dam.	Not allowed; see section 2.3.17.7	Same as Moderate Management	Same as Moderate Management
Small Hydroelectric Power Development Hydroelectric generation by low-head or instream structures that do not change the flow of the river.	May be authorized; see section 2.3.17.7	Not Allowed	Same as Minimal Management

2.4 Implementation and Monitoring

Implementation of this Comprehensive Conservation Plan will be accomplished by means of various step-down plans described in section 2.5. Each of these plans has its own focus and revision schedule.

Part of the implementation process is the Refuges' involvement with partnership opportunities, as discussed in section 2.7.

Monitoring the outcome of implementation is effected by means of surveys, inventories, creel censuses, etc., (section 2.8) and may lead to amendment or revision of the Comprehensive Conservation Plan.

2.5 Step-Down Plans

Step-down management plans are plans that deal with specific management subjects. They describe management strategies and implementation schedules and provide details necessary to fulfill management goals and objectives identified in the Conservation Plan. (DSM 602 FW 1.5).

Step-down plans for these Refuges include the following:

2.5.1 Cultural Resource Guide

This step-down plan provides guidance to refuge staff in meeting legal requirements to protect and manage the cultural resources of the Refuges. The Cultural Resources Guide provides a ready reference to the cultural resource guidance provided by law and regulation, by the Service Manual, and by the Cultural Resource Management Handbook. As a guide, it outlines roles and responsibilities, summarizes legislation governing management of cultural resources, and contains information of potential use to the refuge manager. It describes the current state of our knowledge of prehistory and history of the region. It includes a list of projects that will fill in gaps in knowledge or will complete existing work. The guide was completed in 1996, and the next review is in 2008.

2.5.2 Environmental Education Plan

An environmental education plan gives direction to the educational and outreach programs conducted by refuge staff. Programs are primarily directed at children but include all segments of the populations in the communities surrounding the Refuges. All refuge staff are involved with formal and informal programs that focus on teaching about fish and wildlife and the ecosystems around them. Emphasis is on national directives of the Service, refuge purposes, and special programs such as International Migratory Bird Day, National Wildlife Refuge Week, National Fishing Week, and the Alaska Goose Calendar Contest. Educational programs are promoted through contacts with school faculty, classroom visits, providing environmental education materials, and lending educational materials. The Refuges environmental education plan was initially developed in 1991 and is updated yearly.

2.5.3 Facilities Management Plan

A facilities management plan describes the history and condition of all Service buildings associated with the Refuges. It includes an inventory describing the adequacy of each of the structures for its present use and provides a schedule for future repairs and construction to meet refuge needs. The current plan was approved in January 1997.

2.5.3.1 Refuge Infrastructure

Several of the buildings in use at the King Salmon office compound date to 1939, when the Bureau of Commercial Fisheries established the site. Although some newer buildings have been constructed and others have been updated throughout the years, the facility is dated and not adequate for today's needs. Several buildings do not meet current state building codes. Facilities associated with the Refuges and plans for construction will not vary by alternative. An administrative building at the King Salmon office compound was constructed during 2002 to replace the existing space.

Other off-refuge projects planned for, but not yet scheduled, include the following:

> Construction of new bunkhouse
>
> Construction of a duplex residence
>
> Construction of a maintenance shop at the office compound
>
> Construction or lease of administrative facilities and hangar space in the Chignik Unit
>
> Coordination with partners to ensure that a permanent visitor center facility is provided in King Salmon

Projects planned on the Refuges, but not yet scheduled, include construction or replacement of administrative cabins at Ugashik Narrows or Island Arm and at the Yantarni Bay airstrip. A complete facility inventory and description of needed facilities is presented in the Revised Comprehensive Conservation Plan and Environmental Impact Statement (section 3.6.1).

In addition to refuge-owned administrative facilities, two permitted administrative cabins, owned by the State of Alaska (ADF&G) are within the Refuges: one at Orzinsky Bay and another on the Egegik River near the outlet of Becharof Lake.

2.5.4 Fire Management Plan

Fire management plans describe how a refuge will respond in a wildland fire situation and are normally required by the planning process. A fire management plan is not required for the Alaska Peninsula and Becharof Refuges.

2.5.5 Fisheries Management Plan

The fisheries management plan describes the fishery resource, the ways in which humans have used the resource, the history of fisheries management on the Refuges, and major issues and concerns. The plan provides for continued use of fishery resources by subsistence, commercial, and recreational users. It provides direction to ensure the conservation of fishery resources and habitat. It describes objectives and tasks to address the issues and concerns and assigns priorities and costs for federal tasks. It was last updated in 1994 and is scheduled for review in 2008.

2.5.6 Habitat Inventory Plan

The habitat inventory plan will be developed to guide the Refuges in evaluating habitats by developing goals, objectives, priorities, and methods for conducting habitat inventories. The plan will guide development of maps of major vegetation types and maps and habitat models for caribou, moose, and additional species. It will incorporate a plan for a reconnaissance of invasive plant and animal species. It is expected to be completed by December 2007.

2.5.7 Land-Protection Plan

A land-protection plan (LPP) focuses on private lands within the refuge boundaries with the goal of identifying and conserving high-quality habitat on those lands. The plan will guide the Refuges' land conservation activities and provide a framework for refuge and private landowner cooperation. Any course of action will require mutual consent. The plan does not obligate either the Refuges or the landowners to undertake any of the land-conservation measures identified. The Refuges must consider management goals, priorities, and the availability of funds when approached by private landowners with land-conservation proposals. The Refuges' LPP was completed in 2002.

2.5.8 Public-Use Management Plan or Visitor Services Plan

A public-use management plan (PUMP) guides the management of recreational and subsistence uses, including hunting, trapping, fishing, guiding, camping, photography, sightseeing, hiking, and wildlife viewing. It summarizes how the public was involved in developing issues and alternatives and describes the alternatives that were developed to manage public use. First completed in 1994, the PUMP was updated by being incorporated into the Revised Comprehensive Conservation Plan and Environmental Impact Statement. The Public Use Management Plan presented in Section 2.5 is to be used in conjunction with the Management Policies and Guidelines (Section 2.3).

2.5.9 Safety Plan

A refuge safety plan focuses on the goal of providing a safe and healthful environment for employees and the visiting public. It aims to minimize accidents resulting in injury to employees and the visiting public and to prevent property damage. It describes programs needed to train personnel in how to deal with the environment, materials, and machines that may pose hazards, with the goal of making safety and environmental health an integral part of every task. The safety plan is revised annually.

2.5.10   Water Resources Plan

A water resources plan guides collection of hydrologic data on waters within and draining onto the Refuges. Objectives of this plan are to document the occurrence, quantity, distribution, and movement of surface waters and to quantify instream water rights needed to maintain and protect fish and wildlife habitats. The plan describes the waterbodies of interest and the goals, objectives, priorities, and methods of study needed. A water resources plan for the Refuges is scheduled to be developed by 2010.

2.5.11   Wildlife Inventory Plan

A wildlife inventory plan provides guidance in planning a program to inventory and monitor the animal populations of the Refuges. This plan supports Service policy to collect baseline information, monitor critical parameters and trends, and base management on biologically and statistically sound data. This plan will guide collection of data on species of management concern. It will describe the types of surveys that will be used, emphasis of the studies, sampling design and data standards, reporting requirements, how the data will be stored, and when data will be updated. A wildlife inventory plan for the Refuges expected to be completed by October 2007.

2.5.12   Wilderness Stewardship Plan

This plan is a step-down management plan that provides detailed strategies and implementation schedules for meeting the broader wilderness goals and objectives identified in the Conservation Plan.

A Wilderness stewardship plan guides the preservation, stewardship, and use of a particular Wilderness area. In it are described the goals, objectives, and stewardship strategies for the Wilderness area, based on the refuge purpose(s) (including Wilderness Act purposes), System mission, and wilderness stewardship principles. It contains specific, measurable stewardship objectives that address the preservation of cultural and natural resource values and conditions. This plan must clearly show the strategies and actions to be used and implemented to preserve the wilderness resource and the linkage between those strategies and actions and the wilderness objectives. It also contains indicators, standards, conditions, or thresholds that define adverse impacts on wilderness character and values and that will trigger stewardship actions to reduce or prevent them.

A Wilderness stewardship plan for the Refuges will be completed, in coordination with state wildlife agencies and with public involvement, by 2010.

2.6 Public Use Management Plan

The intent of this section is to clarify and where necessary provide detail to the management direction set forth previously in Section 2.3.

Most visits to the Refuges are for subsistence uses or for hunting, fishing, or other wildlife-dependent recreation. Fixed-wing aircraft landings will not be limited. Airplanes will continue to be allowed to land on sand blows, gravel bars, waterbodies, and the few primitive airstrips that exist. All rivers and lakes will remain open to motorboats. Unless use of helicopters for recreation access within the Becharof Wilderness is determined to have been established prior to refuge establishment, landings for recreation access or use will be prohibited within the Becharof Wilderness and will be considered on a case-by-case basis elsewhere on the Refuges.

Snowmachines and powerboats will be allowed throughout the Refuges. Off-road vehicles will be allowed throughout the Refuges, as provided for in established regulations, for subsistence purposes and could be limited only if necessary to protect resources. Off-road vehicles for recreation and commercial purposes will be limited to established trails in the Yantarni Bay Moderate Management area. No public use cabins or other facilities or hardened trails will be developed for recreation use. Public-use monitoring and management will continue to be mainly reactive, focused on investigating reports of conflicts and impacts.

The opportunity for continued subsistence use is one of the Refuges' purposes and will continue to be a management priority. As specified in the Refuge Improvement Act, wildlife-dependent recreation will be the priority general public use; these recreation activities are defined as hunting, fishing, wildlife viewing, photography, and environmental education and interpretation. These uses will be allowed and facilitated as long as they remained compatible with refuge purposes and the Refuge System mission. Recreation will be managed to provide opportunities for quality experiences, as defined in this Plan and Service policy. State regulations for the harvest of fish and game will continue to take precedence unless the Refuges were closed to such uses by the Federal Subsistence Board.

2.6.1 Wildlife

Bears—All areas will remain open for people to view bears. Detailed public information, including recommendations and precautions for visitors (such as how to behave around bears), will continue to be provided. Areas providing opportunities for viewing bears and other wildlife will be identified. Impacts of use on sensitive bear areas will be monitored.

Seabirds—Under the Migratory Bird Treaty Act, Eskimos and Indians may take, at any season, auks, auklets, guillemots, scoters, murres, and puffins; their eggs for food; and their skins for clothing. The birds and eggs cannot be sold or offered for sale.

Other migratory birds—The 1916 Convention for the Protection of Migratory Birds in Canada and the United States, as implemented by the Migratory Bird Treaty Act, prohibited spring and summer hunting for migratory birds. The treaty called for a closed season in both countries between March 10 and September 1; hunting was allowed under federal and state regulations at other times of the year. In 1997, the treaty was amended to allow subsistence harvest of migratory birds for certain inhabitants of Alaska. In the Bristol Bay region, hunting is allowed for selected waterfowl, seabirds, shorebirds, loons, and owls.

Eagles—Eagles are managed under the Bald Eagle Protection Act and related regulations.

Caribou—Hunting is allowed, subject to state and federal regulations. As of 2005, caribou in game management units 9C and 9E were under state Tier II hunting restrictions, reflecting the decline of the caribou herd.

2.6.2 Access

Pack Animals

The private use of pack animals—such as horses, llamas, or dogs—will be allowed by the general public. As of May 2005, only dogs (both pack dogs and dog teams) are used on the Refuges, although this use is minimal. Commercial use of pack animals on the Refuges will be evaluated on a case-by-case basis; if approved, measures to protect resources and avoid conflict with other users will be included in the special-use permit.

Motorboats

Motorboat access (including jet boats) will be allowed in the Refuges, as specified by ANILCA. Use will be monitored to determine if additional management action is needed.

Aircraft

Aeronautical charts recommend avoiding flight below 2,000 feet above ground level, except during take-off and landing approach. There will be no limits on fixed-wing aircraft landings within the Refuges. Helicopter access for recreation uses will be considered on a case-by-case basis.

Off-Road Vehicles

A winter route over the frozen surface of Big Creek was approved in the Becharof Conservation Plan (but regulations were not developed). Under current state and federal hunting regulations, the Naknek River drainage upstream from and including the King Salmon Creek drainage is closed, from August 1 through November 30, to the use of any motorized vehicle except an aircraft, boat, or snowmachine for hunting; this closure includes transportation of hunters, their hunting gear, and/or parts of game. However, this does not apply to motorized vehicles on the Naknek, King Salmon, Lake Camp, and Rapids Camp roads; on the Pike

Ridge and King Salmon Creek trails; and on the frozen surfaces of the Naknek River and Big Creek.

Off-road vehicle (ORV) use for subsistence (by three- and four-wheeled vehicles with a vehicle weight of 650 pounds or less) will continue to be allowed as specified in 50CFR36.39(c)(2) and will be monitored to ensure there are no adverse effects on Refuges resources. Should adverse effects be detected or appear to be likely in the near future, procedures outlined in 50 CFR 36.12 (U.S. Government 1996-2003) will be followed to take appropriate action.

In the Yantarni Bay Moderate Management area, the airstrip, a trail to the beach, and a trail to the oil well site are designated (on the old gravel roadbeds) for year-round ORV use (Figure 5: Yantarni Bay Moderate Management Area).

Snowmachine access will be allowed when there is adequate snow cover.

Airboats are included in the Service definition of off-road vehicles. They will not be allowed on Refuges lands and waters, but will be allowed on state waters within the boundaries of the Refuges.

2.6.3 Guided and Unguided Public Use

Special-use permits will be required for all commercial uses of the 1985 Refuges, including all types of guiding and air-taxi services. Separate permits will be required for big-game guiding/outfitting and guiding for recreational angling. There will be no limits on the number of air-taxi permits or where air taxis may operate unless a need for such limits was documented through monitoring; additional public involvement will be conducted as part of that process.

Recreation visitors will be encouraged to use areas of the Refuges where subsistence use does not regularly occur. Public use at Becharof Lake outlet, and other locations as appropriate, will be monitored seasonally.

Practice of Leave-No-Trace outdoor ethics will be encouraged. Leave No Trace consists of seven key practices: plan ahead and prepare; travel and camp on durable surfaces; dispose of waste properly; leave what you find; minimize campfire impacts; respect wildlife; and be considerate of other visitors.

Enforceable regulations that address littering, especially littering that attracts bears, will be prepared as needed with input from the state and others. Barrier-free access will be provided at facilities (for example, the visitor center). The Refuges will encourage the guiding industry to provide opportunities for physically challenged visitors.

Other than reserved sites authorized by special-use permits during the fall hunting season (August 1 through November 15), camping will be limited to seven nights per site at the following locations, as specified in 50 CFR Part 36.39(c) (U.S. Government 1996-2003):

> Within one-quarter mile of the shoreline of Becharof Lake in the Severson Peninsula area (Island Arm)
>
> Within one-quarter mile of the shoreline at Becharof Lake outlet
>
> Within one-quarter mile of the shoreline at Ugashik Narrows
>
> Within one-quarter mile of Big Creek
>
> Within one-quarter mile of the shoreline of Gertrude Lake
>
> Within one-quarter mile of Gertrude Creek between Gertrude Lake and the King Salmon River

After seven nights, camps will be required to be moved a minimum of one mile. Impacts of camping elsewhere on the Refuges will be monitored to determine if additional management is necessary. Currently, there are no limits on party size. These camping limits will not apply to subsistence users except at one of the areas: Big Creek. These camping limits also will not apply to state-owned shorelands or tidelands.

Voluntary registration or other special management will be considered for some areas of the Refuges, including the Ukinrek Maars area, archaeological sites, Gertrude Lake, Ruth Lake, old oil wells, and World War II aircraft crash sites. Additional sites could be identified in the future. The purpose of special management will be to ensure that, prior to visiting, people using these areas have appropriate information about the resources and safety precautions.

2.6.4 Big-Game Guiding/Outfitting

In 1992, the Service adopted an Alaska-wide policy for big-game guides/outfitters. The policy established new guide areas and a process for competitively selecting guides to operate within these areas. Implementation began with the 1993 guiding season. As of January 1, 2005, there are 25 big-game guide permittees authorized to operate within the Refuges. The Refuges have the same permit requirements as other Alaska refuges (e.g., requiring guides to report the area and intensity of use). Permits are actively managed; the Refuges staff conducts compliance checks and other oversight actions.

2.6.5 Hunting

As expressed in the Master Memorandum of Understanding (Section 5 - Appendix B of the Revised Comprehensive Conservation Plan and Environmental Impact Statement), the Service recognizes that the state has primary responsibility to manage resident wildlife within the State of Alaska, and the Service will use the state regulatory process to the maximum extent allowed by federal law. If Service restrictions on hunting are needed, they will be done through a rule-making, through closures, or through restrictions under 50CFR 36.41 (2003).

2.6.6 Recreational Fishing and Guided Recreational Fishing

Guided recreational fishing will be authorized within the Refuges. A five-year monitoring program will be developed as staffing and funding levels permit, and its findings will be used to determine any needed additional management actions. New recreational fishing base camps will not be authorized on Refuges lands until the monitoring program had been completed, which is scheduled for 2010.

Limits on the amount of recreational fishing at critical areas (such as the Becharof Lake outlet) could be proposed on an interim basis during the monitoring program if serious problems were detected. Limits will be proposed through regulation of fishing by the Alaska Board of Fisheries. The Service recognizes that the state has primary responsibility to manage fish, and it will use the state regulatory process to the maximum extent allowed by federal law. If special refuge regulations are needed, the Service will implement them through a rule-making, through closures, or through restrictions under 50CFR 36.41 (2003).

Currently, there are no limits on the number of recreational fishing guides authorized. A competitive process will be used to allocate permits in the future if there were a need to limit the number of guides and/or facilities within areas of the Refuges. Improved public information on appropriate fishing techniques—such as catch and release—will be provided.

2.6.7 Facility Development and Use

Trails and Campsites

Trails will not be constructed. Hikers will be encouraged to use certain designated routes with differing levels of challenge, as described in brochures. Hiking in areas where there are no conflicts with wildlife and/or subsistence use will be encouraged. No campsites will be developed within sensitive wildlife areas. Campsites could be hardened and designated if the need is demonstrated.

Easements

The Refuges will work with Service's Division of Realty personnel and local Native corporations to field-check and update the database of ANCSA 17(b) easements, develop GIS maps of easements, and establish signs onsite as needed. Additional direction for easements is described in Section 2.3.13.

Cabins

There will be no public-use cabins. If private cabin permits terminate and if the federal government assumes ownership, cabins will be removed or converted to subsistence use, safety cabins, or administrative cabins. Permits for construction of new cabins will be considered only for subsistence use and will be subject to case-by-case compatibility determinations and environmental analysis.

An administrative cabin will be constructed at the Yantarni Bay airstrip as funding permits. The Refuge has obtained an annual cooperative agreement for administrative use of the Bible Camp facility to run the "Spirit of Becharof Lake" Ecosystem Science Camp.

Temporary Facilities

Use of temporary facilities will be allowed only for the period of activity authorized. Permit holders will be required to report the beginning and end of seasonal occupancy and any period of non-use. Reclamation bonds will be required. Temporary facilities will be required to be screened, to the extent practicable, from general public view and access points. Facilities will be colored to blend into the surrounding landscape as much as possible, but white wall tents will be allowed.

Appropriate food storage methods will be required when the facility is occupied; no food caches will be authorized while the facility is not occupied. Fuel caches could be allowed in compliance with Service policy and in compliance with stipulations in the compatibility determinations. New temporary facilities, other than for subsistence purposes, will be prohibited within one-quarter mile of the Becharof Lake shoreline.

New temporary facilities will be prohibited in some areas because they will constitute a significant expansion of existing facilities, which will be detrimental to the purposes for which the Refuges were established, especially subsistence activities and hunting and fishing (50 CFR 36.39([c][4][ii]; U.S. Government 1996-2003). The following areas receive heavy public use and are located close to communities and/or contain a substantial number of existing facilities:

> Within one-quarter mile of the shoreline of Big Creek
>
> Within one-quarter mile of the shorelines of Gertrude Lake and Long Lake
>
> Within one-quarter mile of the airstrip at the confluence of Gertrude Creek and the King Salmon River
>
> Within one-quarter mile of the shorelines of Upper and Lower Ugashik lakes
>
> Within one-quarter mile of the shoreline of Becharof Lake outlet

2.6.8 Information and Education

Because of the lack of developed visitor facilities on the Refuges, interpretive and educational efforts will occur primarily in King Salmon or in surrounding villages. The Refuges' public-use staff will manage and operate the King Salmon Visitor Center, located in a leased building at the airport in King Salmon, in cooperation with the National Park Service, Bristol Bay Borough, and Lake and Peninsula Borough. The visitor center will be expanded to provide outreach environmental education programs at non-refuge facilities. Land-status information will be available at the visitor center.

The Refuges will have an active education and outreach program. The Refuges will provide a visiting interpreter program at off-refuge facilities such as lodges. Environmental education programs will focus on the National Refuge System, the purposes for which Refuges were established, and significant resource management issues. The Refuges will also promote conservation of geese and waterfowl through the Western Alaska Goose Calendar Contest and the Alaska Junior Federal Duck Stamp Contest. The Refuges will conduct additional programs and activities for special events and occasions such as National Wildlife Refuge week, National Wildlife Week, International Migratory Bird Day, and National Fishing Week.

The environmental education plan is updated yearly. Implementation will be subject to availability of funds. The Refuge Information Technician program will continue.

2.6.9 Commercial Services

Commercial transporters and guides will continue to be administered through special use permits. Big-game hunting guides are limited in number. Twenty-five big-game guide permittees were authorized to operate within the Refuges as of January 1, 2005. There are 21 guide areas on the Refuges (six in Becharof Refuge, seven in Ugashik Unit, and eight in Chignik Unit). Guides may be permitted to hunt in more than one area. Several areas are "joint-use areas" and are used by more than one guide. Guides compete for permits through formal proposals that are evaluated by the Service. Permits for guiding recreational anglers and for commercial transporters are not limited. Proposals for helicopter operations have not been approved in the past, but will be considered on a case-by-case basis.

2.7 Partnership Opportunities

Partnerships with other organizations are among the ways in which the Service fulfills its mission: "Working with others to conserve, protect, and enhance fish, wildlife, and plants and their habitats for the continuing benefit of the American people." Partnership opportunities will be consistent throughout all alternatives.

The Refuges exist within a dynamic ecosystem. Fish, wildlife, and other resources do not respect artificial boundaries, and many of the resources within the Refuges are of national and international importance. The Service recognizes that the public, organizations, and other government agencies have interests in the Refuges. Implementation of many refuge programs requires community involvement and assistance.

2.7.1 Desired Partnerships

The Refuges look for opportunities to coordinate activities with the following, among others:

> Koniag, Inc., the Aleut Corporation, and the Bristol Bay Native Corporation
>
> Local village corporations
>
> Local village councils
>
> Local communities and boroughs
>
> State of Alaska
>
> National Park Service
>
> Universities
>
> Nongovernmental organizations
>
> Alaska Natural History Association (ANHA)

2.7.2 Existing, past, and potential partnerships

Existing, past, and potential partnerships include:

King Salmon Visitor Center, providing information and educational services highlighting the natural and cultural resources and recreation opportunities on the Alaska Peninsula; operated in conjunction with the National Park Service, Bristol Bay Borough, Lake and Peninsula Borough, and the Alaska Natural History Association (ANHA)

"Spirit of Becharof Lake" Ecosystem Science Camp, a week-long residential camp for rural high school students operated in partnership with U.S. Geological Survey (USGS) Alaska Science Center, Bristol Bay School District, Lake and Peninsula School District, Alaska Audubon Society, ANHA, and the Native American Fish and Wildlife Society

Environmental education and outreach programs in coordination with Bristol Bay School District, Lake and Peninsula School District, scouting organizations, traditional village councils, village elders, Alaska Audubon Society, Ducks Unlimited, and Alaska Department of Fish & Game (ADF&G)

Planning for management of fish and wildlife resources on Service lands conducted in cooperation with ADF&G, based on a formal memorandum of understanding

Inventory, monitoring, and study of the Northern Alaska Peninsula caribou herd—including herd counts, composition counts, and calf mortality studies—conducted in formal cooperation with ADF&G

Moose trend surveys to determine population trends and composition conducted in conjunction with ADF&G and the National Park Service

Design, development, and production of refuge-related interpretive education materials in cooperation with ANHA

A creel survey of the sport fishery conducted at the Ugashik Narrows in conjunction with ADF&G

Annual spring breeding birds surveys conducted in conjunction with the National Park Service

Monitoring Avian Productivity and Survivorship (MAPS) continuing studies of bird populations conducted in conjunction with the Institute for Bird Populations

Bird counts conducted several times per year with the cooperation of partners, including the National Audubon Society, Partners in Flight, and USGS's Biological Resources Division

Annual bird banding performed in conjunction with USGS's Biological Resources Division

Participation in planning efforts with gateway communities, including the Bristol Bay Borough, the Lake and Peninsula Borough, and local villages (in recognition that the Refuges are important in the economic and social life of neighboring communities)

Ecoregional plans to identify key habitats and vegetation communities developed for all lands on the Alaska Peninsula, in the cooperation with the Nature Conservancy

Bristol Bay Native Corporation has suggested that the Ugashik Narrows is an area in which it could cooperate with the Service on studies and planning. The Service will be willing to participate in this. The State of Alaska will be included in any planning in this area because of the fishery resource and potential navigability issues.

Studies of archaeological sites at Ugashik Narrows conducted by the University of Oregon

2.8 Monitoring and Evaluation

Monitoring helps refuge staff track the progress of plan implementation. Results of monitoring tell us how well objectives are being achieved and help staff measure progress towards accomplishing goals. Table 3 displays inventory and monitoring projects that will concern fish, wildlife, and bird populations and their habitats. Table 4 displays monitoring indicators for public use.

Monitoring will begin in the year this Plan is approved.

Table 3: Inventory and Monitoring Projects Associated with the Management Direction

Mandates	Resources	Monitor	Potential Measures
Ecosystem Integrity	Water Soils Birds (including neotropical migrants, shorebirds, waterfowl, and raptors) Mammals (game and nongame, furbearers) Reptiles Fish (anadromous and resident) Invertebrates Habitat	Water quality and quantity Erosion Vegetation Species abundance Population dynamics Habitat requirements Habitat quality and quantity Distribution and movements Invasive species User impacts	Water quality (including dissolved oxygen, suspended sediment, turbidity, pH) Gulley formation Flow rate Presence/absence of monitored resource Population range Population trends Population composition Population estimates Population productivity Traditional ecological knowledge Harvest trends Migration patterns Range condition Plant species composition Habitat condition (species-specific) Habitat degradation (species specific)
Subsistence Uses	Game mammals Anadromous fish Resident fish Waterfowl Furbearers Seabirds Habitat		
Other Public Uses	Game mammals Anadromous fish Resident fish Waterfowl Habitat		

Table 4: Monitoring Indicators for Public Use, Standards, and Possible Actions

Monitoring Question	Measured Action and Effect Key Indicator(s)	Management Standard(s) to Be Used	Possible Management Actions Triggered if Standard(s) Not Met	Sampling Procedure and Frequency
What is the nature and extent of conflicts between recreational and subsistence uses at the Becharof Outlet?	Observations of behavior of subsistence and recreational users at the outlet; interviews with a randomly selected subsample of site users. Indicators: reported levels of displacement, competition, crowding, and other sources of conflict. Compare new information with that obtained in 1999 and 2000.	Likelihood of significant impact, if actions not taken, to subsistence users because of displacement, depletion of resources, or other effects of recreational use	To be determined, based on nature of findings. Visitor education; if not successful, possible zoning of recreational use by location or timing. Work cooperatively with State of Alaska.	Three years out of 10; more if needed based on results. Observations during coho season; interviews with randomly selected site users

Monitoring Question	Measured Action and Effect Key Indicator(s)	Management Standard(s) to Be Used	Possible Management Actions Triggered if Standard(s) Not Met	Sampling Procedure and Frequency
Is off-road vehicle (ORV) use causing adverse effects on refuge resources?	*Vegetation and soil damage*		Designating areas or trails for use and limiting use in undesignated areas Designating times of year or seasons that travel will be permitted in areas open to ORV use Closing certain areas of impact for parts of seasons or whole years until recovery can produce desired results Developing cooperative management and enforcement strategies with other state, private, and federal entities that are operating in the area(s) of concern	Use aerial surveys and photo points to look for visible changes; conduct biannually Staff observations and user contacts; ongoing effort with information compiled annually
	Visible wear to trails Surface rutting Laying over or breaking of vegetation Point erosion to water bodies	Visible increase for more than one season Visible increase Visible or documented point-source erosion from ORV use Documented increase (amount to be determined) in conflicts between ORV users and other users for more than one season		

Monitoring Question	Measured Action and Effect Key Indicator(s)	Management Standard(s) to Be Used	Possible Management Actions Triggered if Standard(s) Not Met	Sampling Procedure and Frequency
Is recreational use of sensitive wildlife areas affecting brown bears?	*Bear incidents*		Increased visitor education efforts; close specific areas to camping and/or visitation during critical bear-use periods; additional regulation of visitors viewing bears; work cooperatively with ADF&G	Reports of incidents; compiled annually.
	Defense of life or property (DLP) kills	Increase in number of incidents at specific locations Increase in one season or over several seasons.		Reports of DLP kills; compiled annually
	Change in distribution or numbers in specific stream reaches, sedge meadows, etc.	Decrease in local distribution or numbers of bears correlated to increase in public use		Distribution and number of bears per mile of habitat; inventoried locally
Is recreational use of the Becharof Lake area displacing subsistence users?	Reported displacement	Upward trends in reports of displacement	Increase visitor education; work with guides, transporters, and subsistence users to resolve; recommend changes to state and federal hunting regulations	Number and type of incidents observed and/or reported; compiled annually
Is recreational use of the Refuges displacing subsistence users?	Reported displacement	Upward trends in reports of displacement	Increase visitor education; work with guides, transporters, and subsistence users to resolve; recommend changes to state and federal hunting regulations	Number and type of incidents observed and/or reported; compiled annually

Monitoring Question	Measured Action and Effect Key Indicator(s)	Management Standard(s) to Be Used	Possible Management Actions Triggered if Standard(s) Not Met	Sampling Procedure and Frequency
Are dispersed campsites affecting soils and vegetation?	Soil and vegetation condition	Visible or measurable damage to tundra over more than 10% of site: >1 square meter of bare ground or compacted (puddled) soils; other(s) to be developed	Increased user education efforts; revegetate site; designate or harden campsite; close site to camping	Campsite inventory and re-inventory of ground cover disturbance; frequency to be determined
What is the current level of visitor use in key areas of the Refuges, and what are the trends?	Number of visitors, number of parties, length of stay, sites visited, activities occurring on the Refuges	Not applicable; baseline data	Monitoring to collect baseline information; will trigger visitor-use studies at specific sites as needed	Guide reports, air-taxi operator reports, staff observations; compiled annually
What are the current amounts and distributions of recreational fishing activities on the Refuges, and what are the effects of this use?	Recreational fishing locations, fishing pressure, fish population conditions and trends, and conflicts	To be developed (see below for one component)	Recommend changes in fishing regulations to Alaska Board of Fisheries; limit recreational fishing access to key sites where there are problems; allocate recreational fishing access between guided and nonguided visitors; develop plan for management of recreational fishing, as necessary	Guide reports, air-taxi operator reports, visitor contacts, creel surveys, mail-in state surveys; five-year study; data compiled annually

Monitoring Question	Measured Action and Effect Key Indicator(s)	Management Standard(s) to Be Used	Possible Management Actions Triggered if Standard(s) Not Met	Sampling Procedure and Frequency
Is quality of recreation being maintained at key recreational fishing sites?	Visitor perceptions of quality and resource and social conditions, with pilot survey beginning at the Ugashik Narrows and other sites as needed (determined from baseline data collection above)	Statistically determined, based on survey results	Develop site objectives; work with air taxis and recreational fishing guides to voluntarily meet objectives; work with State of Alaska to regulate activity levels (only if objectives cannot be met through other methods)	Random sample survey of approximately 75 guided and 75 nonguided anglers annually for three years
Are opportunities for primitive and unconfined recreation still present in the Becharof Wilderness and other areas recommended for Wilderness designation?	Visitor perceptions of opportunities for solitude and other characteristics of primitive recreation	95% or more of recreation visitors have what they define as a primitive experience	Visitor education and voluntary redistribution of trips; regulation of use levels a possibility over the long term but only if use levels and/or its social impacts increase substantially over present levels	Random sample mail survey of visitors to the Wilderness and areas recommended for Wilderness designation (n=100) every three years
Are guides following procedures outlined in special-use permits?	Compliance with permit stipulations	100% compliance	Modifications to procedures; standard disciplinary actions that can be taken under existing regulations	Field check of each permit-holder once or more annually in the field

2.9 Plan Amendment and Revision

Periodic review and revision of the Comprehensive Conservation Plan will be necessary. As knowledge of the Refuges resources and users improves, changes in management directions may be identified. Fish and wildlife populations, user groups, adjacent land users, and other management considerations change with time, often in unforeseen ways. Problems also may be encountered in implementing that Plan.

Revisions are a necessary part of the adaptive management approach used by the Refuges. This means that objectives and strategies to reach goals can be adjusted. Most of the resulting changes will fine-tune the management direction. Minor changes will not require modification of the Comprehensive Conservation Plan as they will be addressed in the step-down plans and annual work plans. If a significant change is required in the management of the Refuges it would become necessary to revise the Comprehensive Conservation Plan.

To enable refuge users; adjacent landowners; local, state and federal agencies, and other interested parties to express their views on how the Refuges are being managed, the Refuges will periodically hold meetings—or use other techniques such as comment cards and surveys—to solicit comments for evaluation purposes. By encouraging continuing public input, the Refuges will be better able to serve the public, to determine potential problems before they occur, and to take immediate action to resolve existing problems.

Every three to five years, Refuges staff will review public comments, local and state government recommendations, staff recommendations, research studies, and other sources to determine if revisions to the Comprehensive Conservation Plan are necessary. If major changes are proposed, public meetings may be held or new environmental assessment and environmental impact statements may be necessary. Full review and updating of the Comprehensive Conservation Plan will occur every 15 years.

3. References

Bayha, K., S. Lyons, and M.L. Harle. 1997. "Strategic Plan for Water Resources Branch." WRB-97-1. Anchorage, Alaska: U.S. Department of the Interior, Fish & Wildlife Service, Division of Realty. 25 pp.

DOI. 2001. "Departmental Manual." Accessed November 13, 2003. At `http://elips.doi.gov/app_dm/index.cfm?fuseaction=home` on the World Wide Web, produced by U.S. Department of the Interior. Source last updated December 1, 2001.

USDI. 2001. "Department of the Interior--Alaska Policy on Government-to-Government Relations with Alaska Native Tribes." Washington, D.C: U.S. Department of the Interior. 3 pp. (Policy signed on January 18, 2001.)

USFWS. 1973. "The Endangered Species Act of 1973." Accessed October 4, 2004. At `http://endangered.fws.gov/esa.html` on the World Wide Web, produced by U.S. Fish & Wildlife Service. Source last updated March 20, 2001.

USFWS. 1985. "Becharof National Wildlife Refuge." Final Comprehensive Conservation Plan, wilderness review, and environmental impact statement. Anchorage, Alaska: U.S. Department of the Interior, Fish & Wildlife Service.

USFWS. 1985a. Alaska Peninsula National Wildlife Refuge Final Comprehensive Conservation Plan, Environmental Impact Statement, and Wilderness Review. Anchorage, Alaska: U.S. Fish & Wildlife Service. 426 pp.

USFWS. 1985b. Becharof National Wildlife Refuge Final Comprehensive Conservation Plan, Environmental Impact Statement, and Wilderness Review. Anchorage, Alaska: U.S. Fish & Wildlife Service.

USFWS. 1987. "Alaska Peninsula National Wildlife Refuge Draft Wilderness Amendment and Supplemental Environmental Impact Statement." Anchorage, Alaska: U.S. Fish & Wildlife Service. 171 pages.

USFWS. 1988. Alaska Maritime National Wildlife Refuge Final Comprehensive Conservation Plan, Wilderness Review, and Environmental Impact Statement. Anchorage, Alaska: U.S. Fish & Wildlife Service.

USFWS. 1992. "Cultural Resources Handbook." Accessed June 4, 2003, 2003. At http://www.policy.fws.gov/614fw1.html on the

USFWS. 1992. "Cultural Resources Handbook." Accessed October 4, 2004. At `http://policy.fws.gov/614fw1.html` on the World Wide Web, produced by U.S. Fish & Wildlife Service. Source last updated November 1992.

USFWS. 1994a. "Alaska Peninsula/Becharof National Wildlife Refuge Complex Final Public Use Management Plan." Anchorage, Alaska: U.S. Fish & Wildlife Service.

USFWS. 1994b. "Native American Policy." National Policy Issuance #94-10. Washington, D.C: U.S. Fish & Wildlife Service. 11 pp. (Policy signed on June 28, 1994; issued as national policy on August 24, 1994.)

USFWS. "Service Manual." Accessed June 4, 2003. At http://policy.fws.gov/manual.html on the World Wide Web, produced by U.S. Fish & Wildlife Service.

USFWS. "Service Manual." Accessed October 4, 2004. At http://policy.fws.gov/manual.html on the World Wide Web, produced by U.S. Fish & Wildlife Service.

U.S. Government. 1996-2003. "Code of Federal Regulations." Accessed October 4, 2004. At http://www.gpoaccess.gov/cfr/index.html on the World Wide Web, produced by Office of the Federal Register, National Archives and Records Administration. Source last updated April 14, 2003.

U.S. Government. 1996-2003. "Code of Federal Regulations." Accessed August 30, 2005. At http://www.gpoaccess.gov/cfr/index.html on the World Wide Web, produced by Office of the Federal Register, National Archives and Records Administration. Source last updated March 10, 2005.

4. Appendix A:
Special Values

ANILCA Section 304(g) states that, before developing or revising a Comprehensive Conservation Plan, "the special values of the refuge, as well as any other archaeological, cultural, ecological, geological, historical, paleontological, scenic, or wilderness value of the refuge" should be identified. The following discussion describes the special values that have been identified for the Alaska Peninsula and Becharof Refuges. (Refer to Figure 2: Becharof National Wildlife Refuge, 3, and 4)

4.1.1 Refuge Characteristics Valued by the Public

Public comment indicated that people valued the naturalness of the Refuges, their wildness and wilderness qualities, wildlife in its natural diversity, the naturally functioning ecosystems, and the associated wildlife-related recreation opportunities.

4.1.2 Becharof Refuge

4.1.2.1 Becharof Wilderness Area

The Becharof Wilderness Area was established in 1980 by ANILCA. It is bounded on the north by the designated Wilderness of the Katmai National Park and Preserve and by the Kejulik Pinnacles, on the west by Becharof Lake, and on the east and south by the Pacific Ocean.

The rugged Kejulik Pinnacles and Aleutian Mountains, separated by the broad Kejulik River valley provide spectacular scenery. The Pacific coast has towering cliffs where the mountains meet the sea.

The area supports a variety of intact and functioning plant and animal communities. Some of the world's largest salmon runs spawn in the Becharof Lake watershed, which includes much of this Wilderness Area. The area supports populations of brown bear, wolves, moose, caribou, and numerous other species. Cliffs on the Pacific coast support large seabird colonies.

The Becharof Wilderness Area includes portions of areas described subsequently as the Becharof Ecosystem, Becharof and Katmai Uplands, and Seabird Colonies.

4.1.2.2 Becharof Ecosystem

Becharof Lake is the second-largest lake in Alaska. The lake and its drainage support one of the largest sockeye salmon runs in Bristol Bay as well as a large suite of sockeye predators, including char, Arctic grayling, brown bears, cormorants, terns, and bald eagles. The uplands within this ecosystem provide habitat for moose, caribou, nesting waterfowl and songbirds, small mammals, and other species within a rich matrix of vegetation types. The outlet of Becharof Lake is popular with subsistence fishermen and recreation anglers. Significant paleontological resources have been located in the fossil-rich uplands, including fossils of a pliosaur (a giant marine reptile from the late Jurassic period) found in the Kejulik drainage. The area has special scenic and public-use values.

4.1.2.3 Island Arm and Ruth Lake

The Island Arm of Becharof Lake provides most of the spawning and rearing habitat for sockeye salmon within the Becharof drainage. Consequently, it hosts one of the highest densities of brown bear feeding on spawning salmon that occurs in Becharof Refuge and in the Ugashik Unit. Island Arm is also especially scenic, with its many small islands and surrounding mountains. Among them, Ruth Lake and River provide outstanding examples, even by Alaska Peninsula standards, of beautiful glaciated mountain drainages.

4.1.2.4 Becharof and Katmai Uplands

These uplands on the eastern boundary of the refuge support important brown bear denning and moose winter range. The area is one of the most scenic parts of the refuge.

4.1.2.5 Mt. Peulik and Gas Rocks Area

This area is geologically significant, being one of Alaska's most recent volcanically active sites. The 1977 eruption which created the Ukinrek Maars received international attention. In addition to its scientific and educational values, the area has special scenic values. At 4,835 feet the classic volcanic cone of Mt. Peulik, which last erupted in 1852, dominates the area. The cinder cones of the Ugashik Caldera complete this unique volcanic landscape.

4.1.2.6 King Salmon River Drainage (Becharof)

This drainage provides important spawning and rearing habitat for Chinook, coho, chum, and pink salmon. It contains significant Dolly Varden char and Arctic grayling populations and the farthest-south resident population of rainbow trout on the Alaska Peninsula. The area provides brown bear, moose, and caribou habitat as well as nesting habitat for tundra swans, sandhill cranes, ptarmigan, and other birds. It is important for local subsistence and for recreational angling and hunting.

4.1.2.7 Big Creek Drainage

This area is important for salmon spawning and rearing and includes key moose, caribou, and brown bear habitats. It is one of the most heavily visited parts of the Refuges for subsistence purposes and is a favorite trapping area for local residents. Recreational hunting for moose and caribou is popular.

4.1.2.8 Kanatak Village

Two sites on the Refuges are listed in the Alaska Heritage Resource Survey: the village of Kanatak on Portage Bay and a Russian Orthodox church at the same location. In 1890, Kanatak had 23 residents. In the 1930s, the population expanded to 134 because of oil exploration. This activity ceased in the 1950s and the village was abandoned. In 1981, the church and much of the village were destroyed by fire. These sites are being studied for inclusion in the National Register of Historic Places.

4.1.2.9 Seabird Colonies

Three large colonies of cliff-nesting seabirds in Puale and Dry bays host tens of thousands of murres and thousands of kittiwakes, as well as scores of cormorants and puffins. These are the only murre colonies between the Barren and Semidi islands, a distance of 250 miles. The cliffs provide habitat from which seabirds can use forage resources of the southwestern end of the Shelikof Strait. These colonies and the marine resources were impacted by the 1989 *Exxon Valdez* oil spill.

4.1.3 Alaska Peninsula Refuge

The Alaska Peninsula Refuge (Figure 3: Ugashik Unit, Alaska Peninsula National Wildlife Refuge) contains many unique geologic and scenic features. Indeed, the Alaska Peninsula Refuge is the most scenically diverse of the Bristol Bay refuges: the interplay of volcanic activity with shoreline erosion and glacial scour has created outstanding scenery. The Joint Federal–State Land Use Planning Commission listed Chiginagak and Veniaminof volcanoes, Castle Cape, and the Pacific Coast as making up one of the outstanding scenic complexes of Alaska (Gordon and Shaine 1978). The Ugashik and Chignik units of the Alaska Peninsula Refuge also provide pristine habitat to significant fish and wildlife resources and offer many subsistence and recreation opportunities.

4.1.3.1 Pacific Coast

In addition to its scenic value, the spectacularly rugged Pacific coast—with its cliffs, bays, fjords, and streams—supports a diversity of fish and wildlife resources. These include nesting bald eagles; at least eight nesting species of seabirds, including puffins, cormorants, kittiwakes, and guillemots; and wintering waterfowl such as emperor geese, harlequin ducks, and the threatened Steller's eider.

Five species of Pacific salmon spawn in the coastal drainages, including the commercially significant sockeye run in the Chignik system. Harbor seals, sea otters, and Steller sea lions of the threatened western population haul out along the coast. Local residents report that gray whales enter the refuge boundary in spring to feed in Chignik Lagoon.

Brown bears forage in coastal sedge meadows in spring and in coastal drainages for spawning salmon in summer and fall. More than a thousand caribou summer in coastal drainages and mountains of the Pacific coast of the Ugashik Unit. Moose are common.

Frequent fog, rain, and wind contribute to the beauty of the coast that becomes spectacular on clear days when glacier-covered volcanoes can be seen rising above the steep walls of coastal drainages that meet the sea on rocky coasts. Exemplary streams are the short drainages of Agripina and Port Wrangell Rivers, which flow from glaciers to valley floors, decorated with small lakes and rock outcrops, before draining into rocky bays.

4.1.3.2 Ugashik Lakes

The Ugashik Lakes are world-renowned for trophy Arctic grayling fishing (the Alaska record was set here); the lakes also support large concentrations of lake trout, provide key feeding habitat for brown bears, and provide spawning and rearing habitat for large numbers of sockeye and coho salmon. The Ugashik Narrows has outstanding recreation opportunities for angling for trophy Arctic grayling and other popular sport fish. The Narrows is a unique geologic feature on the Alaska Peninsula, where two of the largest lakes in the area are joined by a shallow, flowing narrows. The Narrows was also important to pre-contact Native communities.

4.1.3.3 Dog Salmon River, Mother Goose Lake, and King Salmon River (Ugashik)

These drainages constitute a major portion of the high-quality winter moose habitat on the central Alaska Peninsula. Stands of poplar are scattered throughout this area, culminating in the only forest (located at Mother Goose Lake and along King Salmon River) southwest of Katmai National Park and Preserve. This forest provides locally unique habitat to many species of breeding songbirds and to hares and lynx. These drainages include a substantial portion of the limited nesting range of the Alaska subspecies of the marbled godwit (Gibson and Kessel 1989; North *et al.* 1996; North and Tucker 1992). The drainages also support runs of five species of Pacific salmon as well as resident populations of Arctic char, Dolly Varden, and other species. Both drainages originate in the glaciers and snowfields of Mt. Kialagvik, Mt. Chiginagak, and surrounding mountains, which provide spectacular scenic backgrounds to the Dog Salmon River meandering through the marshes and to beautiful Mother Goose Lake.

4.1.3.4 Black Lake–Chignik Lake Area

The Black Lake–Chignik Lake area hosts one of the densest seasonal concentrations of brown bears in North America. The tributaries of the Chignik and Alex rivers provide the best examples on the Refuges of high concentrations of spawning sockeye salmon and the large numbers of brown bears they attract. As many as 500 bears congregate on these streams during August (Hicks 1996). Although examples of these interactions are found on other rivers on the Alaska Peninsula, the size of these salmon runs and the number of bears that depend on them are truly exemplary.

4.1.3.5 Castle Cape

Castle Cape consists of extremely rugged mountains deeply indented by the sea; the rocks exhibit a pattern of contrasting dark and light layers that is so pronounced that the cape serves as a famous landmark to ships.

4.1.3.6 Mount Veniaminof

Mount Veniaminof, one of Alaska's active volcanoes, last erupted in 2005. The volcano is massive, with a base diameter of about 30 miles and a summit crater circumference of about 20 miles. In 1967, Mount Veniaminof was designated as a national natural landmark. The spectacular Upper Sandy River originates in the glaciers of Veniaminof and flows through a still-raw volcanic landscape before forming a delta at Sandy Lake.

4.1.4 Alaska Maritime Refuge

4.1.4.1 Seal Cape

Seal Cape is a headland extending from the Alaska Peninsula. The cape provides nesting areas for numerous bird species including; cormorants, black-legged kittiwakes, glaucous-winged gulls, and murrelets. Its extremely rugged coastline is deeply indented by fjord like bays. Cliffs, reaching heights of more than 2,000 feet, line much of the coastline. The scenery is spectacular, with fjords and deeply cut bays set against a backdrop of jagged peaks and pinnacles. This area is very rugged and remote; it provides outstanding opportunities for solitude and primitive recreation.

5. Appendix B: Easements, Withdrawals, and Asserted Rights of Way

5.1 Easements reserved by the Service over private lands under Sec. 17(b) of ANCSA

Section 17(b) of the Alaska Native Claims Settlement Act (ANCSA) authorizes the Secretary of the Interior to reserve public easements on lands conveyed to Native corporations to guarantee access to public lands. These easements include linear easements across Native lands and waters and site easements. These easements are depicted on Figure 9. The following are listed by easement identification number (EIN).

5.1.1 *Ugashik Unit*

SITES (one acre)

EIN 1a C4	Dog Salmon River at north [right] bank in T32S R50W, Sec. 3

5.1.2 *Chignik Unit*

SITES (one acre)

EIN 2 D9	Ivanof Bay at north [left] bank of unnamed slough in T50S R66W, Sec. 18
EIN 2b D9	Chignik River at east [left] bank in T43S R61W, Sec. 32
EIN 2d D9	Portage Bay in T46S R60W, Sec. 15
EIN 2e D9	Chignik River at south [right] bank in T45S R60W, Sec. 30
EIN 5a C5	Anchor Bay at east [left] bank of Red Bluff Creek in T49S R63W, Sec. 22
EIN 9a C5	Bay east of Perryville in T49S R64W, Sec. 26
EIN 20a C4	Black Lake in T43S R61W, Sec. 5
EIN 25a	One-acre site on right bank of Chignik River south of Bearskin Creek with a 25-foot-wide easement on the bed of the Chignik River in T44S R61W, Sec. 32

TRAILS

EIN 1 D9	50 feet wide: Black Lake southerly to Chignik Lake along east [left] bank of Chignik River
EIN 7 C5	25 feet wide: village of Chignik Lake southwesterly to southern arm of Chignik Lake in T46S R61W, Sec. 4
EIN 23	50 feet wide: From EIN 20b to Cathedral Creek floodplain and public land in T44S R61W, Sec. 9

PROPOSED TRAILS (25 feet wide)

EIN 3 D9	Site EIN 2 D9 at Ivanof Bay, westerly along north [left] bank of unnamed slough to T50S R67W, Sec. 23—"Granville Portage"
EIN 5 C5	Site EIN 5a C5 at Anchor Bay, northwesterly parallel to east [left] bank of Red Bluff Creek to T48S R63W, Sec. 9
EIN 7 C4	T50S R67W, Sec. 21, northerly along east [left] bank of unnamed stream to T49S R67W, Sec. 10
EIN 9 C5	Site EIN 9a C5 at bay east of Perryville, northwesterly parallel to south [right] bank of Kametolook River to T48S R64W, Sec. 21
EIN 13 E	Port Heiden, southerly parallel to coastline to north bank of Meshik River, southeasterly to T40S R58W, Sec. 6
EIN 17 C5	Site EIN 2e D9 at Chignik River, southerly to T46S R60W, Sec. 6
EIN 18 C4	Site EIN 2d D9 at Chignik River, northwesterly to T46S R60W, Sec. 9
EIN 20b C4	Site EIN 20a C4 at Black Lake, northeasterly to T42S R61W, Sec. 33
EIN 22 C4	Chignik River in T44S R61W, Sec. 8, southeasterly along Chiaktuck Creek to T44S R61W, Sec. 15
EIN 25	Proposed trail from the right bank of the Chignik River, east to public lands in T44S R62W, Sec. 36

AIRSTRIPS (250' x 3,000')

EIN 5b D9	Chignik River at Black Lake in T43S R61W, Sec. 32

WITHDRAWALS

There are no federal withdrawals within the Refuges.

5.2 Asserted RS-2477 Rights-of-Way

The State of Alaska has identified the following routes that it believes qualify as highways under Revised Statute (RS) 2477, a section of the Mining Act of 1866, which states, "The right-of-way for the construction of highways over public lands, not reserved for public uses, is hereby granted." In addition to specific routes, the

State of Alaska also claims that the section-line easements are RS-2477 rights-of-way. RS-2477 was repealed by the Federal Land Policy and Management Act of 1976, subject to valid existing claims.

Table 5 displays the mileage of asserted RS-2477 routes within the Refuges. Figure 10 displays the locations of asserted RS-2477 routes within and near the Refuges.

Table 5: Mileage of proposed RS 2477 routes within the Refuges.

State Number	Name	FWS	Native Conveyed	Native Selected	Conflict	Private Patent	Total
68	Egegik–Kanatak Trail	47.25	0.00	2.37	0.00	0.00	49.62
221	Egegik–Cold (Puale) Bay Trail	82.82	0.00	0.00	0.00	0.00	82.82
282	Island Bay–Salmon Creek Trail	4.11	0.00	0.00	0.00	0.00	4.11
367	Portage Bay–Mt. Demian Oil Camp Trail	19.16	0.00	5.41	0.00	0.00	24.57
394	Chignik Lagoon–Aniakchak River Trail	18.72	12.47	2.45	0.95	0.32	34.91
1176	Kanatak–Becharof Lake Trail	8.48	0.00	0.31	0.00	0.00	8.79
	1973 DNR Trail Inventory Map "highways" (3)	8.64	2.75	0.16	0.00	0.58	12.13
Total		189.18	15.22	10.70	0.95	0.90	216.95

6. Appendix C:
Species Lists

This appendix includes a list of species for the Alaska Peninsula and Becharof National Wildlife Refuges. The table uses a number of abbreviations, defined as follows:

? = possible/may be probable

BB = Bristol Bay

BRD = Breeder

WTR = Winter resident

MAR BRD = Marginal breeder; for example, found in the boreal in King Salmon and Katmai. Known boreal area is on edge of Becharof National Wildlife Refuge (NWR) (Big Creek drainage), so species probably found there, but on edge of range.

RES = Resident (year-round)

MIG = Migrant (a regular user during the spring or fall migration different from TRAN or INC)

NSHR = Nearshore; i.e., found on offshore islands (for example, belonging to the Alaska Maritime National Wildlife Refuge) or in ocean waters near shore, but not known to use "above mean high tide" on the Refuges

TRAN = Transient: A species where the majority of the population does not regularly breed or migrate through an area, but individuals of the species occasionally pass through the area. The species' winter and/or summer range may lie near the Refuges, which accounts for these occasional strays. Transients are found more often than are accidentals.

ACC = Accidental: A species where the breeding and wintering ranges are distant from the Refuges, but where individuals of the species have been documented on the Refuges. Note that many of the ACC are Asiatic species.

Common Name	Scientific Name	Class/Order/Family	Type/Residence
FISHES—RESIDENT			
Arctic lamprey	*Lampetra japonica*	Cephalaspidomorphi/Petromyzontiformes/Petromyzontidae	Freshwater/Anadromous
Longnose sucker	*Catostomus catostomus*	Actinopterygii/Cypriniformes/Castomidae	Freshwater
Least Cisco	*Coregonus sardinella*	Actinopterygii/Salmoniformes/Salmonidae	Freshwater/Anadromous
Lake Whitefish	*Coregonus clupeaformis*	Actinopterygii/Salmoniformes/Salmonidae	Freshwater
Pygmy Whitefish	*Prosopium coulteri*	Actinopterygii/Salmoniformes/Salmonidae	Freshwater
Round Whitefish	*Prosopium cylindraceum*	Actinopterygii/Salmoniformes/Salmonidae	Freshwater
Lake Trout	*Salvelinus namaycush*	Actinopterygii/Salmoniformes/Salmonidae	Freshwater
Arctic Char	*Salvelinus alpinus*	Actinopterygii/Salmoniformes/Salmonidae	Freshwater
Dolly Varden	*Salvelinus malma*	Actinopterygii/Salmoniformes/Salmonidae	Freshwater/Anadromous
Rainbow Trout/Steelhead	*Oncorhynchus mykiss*	Actinopterygii/Salmoniformes/Salmonidae	Freshwater/Anadromous
Arctic Grayling	*Thymallus arcticus*	Actinopterygii/Salmoniformes/Salmonidae	Freshwater
Pond Smelt	*Hypomesus olidus*	Actinopterygii/Osmeriformes/Osmeridae	Freshwater
Slimy Sculpin	*Cottus cognatus*	Actinopterygii/Scorpaeniformes/Cottidae	Freshwater
Coastrange Sculpin	*Cottus aleuticus*	Actinopterygii/Scorpaeniformes/Cottidae	Freshwater/Brackish
Alaska Blackfish	*Dallia pectoralis*	Actinopterygii/Esociformes/Umbridae	Freshwater
Northern Pike	*Esox lucius*	Actinopterygii/Esociformes/Esocidae	Freshwater
Burbot	*Lota lota*	Actinopterygii/Gadiformes/Lotidae	Freshwater
Three-spined Stickleback	*Gasterosteus aculeatus*	Actinopterygii/Gasterosteiformes/Gasterosteidae	Freshwater/Brackish/Marine
Nine-spined Stickleback	*Pungitius pungitius*	Actinopterygii/Gasterosteiformes/Gasterosteidae	Freshwater/Brackish
FISHES—ANADROMOUS			
Pink Salmon	*Oncorhynchus gorbuscha*	Actinopterygii/Salmoniformes/Salmonidae	Anadromous
Sockeye Salmon	*Oncorhynchus nerka*	Actinopterygii/Salmoniformes/Salmonidae	Anadromous
Chinook Salmon	*Oncorhynchus tschawytscha*	Actinopterygii/Salmoniformes/Salmonidae	Anadromous
Coho Salmon	*Oncorhynchus kisutch*	Actinopterygii/Salmoniformes/Salmonidae	Anadromous
Chum Salmon	*Oncorhynchus keta*	Actinopterygii/Salmoniformes/Salmonidae	Anadromous
Eulachon	*Thaleichthys pacificus*	Actinopterygii/Osmeriformes/Osmeridae	Anadromous

Common Name	Scientific Name	Class/Order/Family	Type/Residence
Rainbow Smelt	Osmerus mordax	Actinopterygii/Osmeriformes/Osmeridae	Anadromous
Pacific Lamprey	Entosphenus tridentatus	Cephalaspidomorphi/Petromyzontiformes/Petromyzontidae	Anadromous
FISHES—MARINE			
Pacific Herring	Clupea harengus pallasii	Actinopterygii/Cluperiformes/Cluperidae	Marine
Surf Smelt	Hypomesus pretiosus	Actinopterygii/Osmeriformes/Osmeridae	Marine
Saffron Cod	Eleginu gracilis	Actinopterygii/Gadiformes/Gadidae	Marine/Brackish/Freshwater
Pacific Staghorn Sculpin	Leptocottus armatus	Actinopterygii/Scorpaeniformes/Cottidae	Brackish/Marine
Sharpnose Sculpin	Clinocotus acuticeps	Actinopterygii/Scorpaeniformes/Cottidae	Marine/Brackish/Freshwater
Starry Flounder	Platichthys stellatus	Actinopterygii/Pleuronectiformes/Pleuronectidae	Marine/Brackish/Freshwater
Fourhorn Sculpin	Myoxocephalus quadricornis	Actinopterygii/Scorpaeniformes/Cottidae	Marine/Brackish
AMPHIBIAN			
Wood Frog	Rana sylvatica	Amphibia/Anura/Ranidae	RES
BIRDS—BREEDING		123 TOTAL (includes marginals)	
Red-throated Loon	Gavia stellata	Aves/Gaviiformes/Gaviidae	BRD
Pacific Loon	Gavia pacifica	Aves/Gaviiformes/Gaviidae	BRD/WTR
Common Loon	Gavia immer	Aves/Gaviiformes/Gaviidae	BRD
Double-crested Cormorant	Phalacrocorax auritus	Aves/Pelecaniformes/Phalacrocoracidae	BRD/WTR?
Red-faced Cormorant	Phalacrocorax urile	Aves/Pelecaniformes/Phalacrocoracidae	BRD/WTR
Pelagic Cormorant	Phalacrocorax pelagicus	Aves/Pelecaniformes/Phalacrocoracidae	BRD/WTR
Greater White-fronted Goose	Anser albifrons	Aves/Anseriformes/Anatidae	BRD
Canada Goose	Branta canadensis occidentalis	Aves/Anseriformes/Anatidae	BRD
Tundra Swan	Cygnus columbianus	Aves/Anseriformes/Anatidae	BRD/WTR

Common Name	Scientific Name	Class/Order/Family	Type/Residence
Gadwall	*Anas strepera*	Aves/Anseriformes/Anatidae	BRD
American Wigeon	*Anas americana*	Aves/Anseriformes/Anatidae	BRD
Mallard	*Anas platyrhynchos*	Aves/Anseriformes/Anatidae	BRD
Northern Shoveler	*Anas clypeata*	Aves/Anseriformes/Anatidae	BRD
Northern Pintail	*Anas acuta*	Aves/Anseriformes/Anatidae	BRD
Green-winged Teal	*Anas crecca*	Aves/Anseriformes/Anatidae	BRD
Greater Scaup	*Aythya marila*	Aves/Anseriformes/Anatidae	BRD/WTR
Common Eider	*Somateria mollissima*	Aves/Anseriformes/Anatidae	BRD/WTR
Harlequin Duck	*Histrionicus histrionicus*	Aves/Anseriformes/Anatidae	BRD/RES
Black Scoter	*Melanitta nigra*	Aves/Anseriformes/Anatidae	BRD/RES
Common Goldeneye	*Bucephala clangula*	Aves/Anseriformes/Anatidae	BRD/RES
Common Merganser	*Mergus merganser*	Aves/Anseriformes/Anatidae	BRD/RES
Red-breasted Merganser	*Mergus serrator*	Aves/Anseriformes/Anatidae	BRD
Osprey	*Pandion haliaetus*	Aves/Falconiformes/Accipitridae	MAR BRD
Bald Eagle	*Haliaeetus leucocephalus*	Aves/Falconiformes/Accipitridae	BRD/RES
Northern Harrier	*Circus cyaneus*	Aves/Falconiformes/Accipitridae	BRD
Northern Goshawk	*Accipiter gentilis*	Aves/Falconiformes/Accipitridae	BRD
Rough-legged Hawk	*Buteo lagopus*	Aves/Falconiformes/Accipitridae	BRD
Golden Eagle	*Aquila chrysaetos*	Aves/Falconiformes/Accipitridae	BRD/RES
Merlin	*Falco columbarius*	Aves/Falconiformes/Falconidae	BRD
Gyrfalcon	*Falco rusticolus*	Aves/Falconiformes/Falconidae	BRD
Peregrine Falcon	*Falco peregrinus*	Aves/Falconiformes/Falconidae	BRD
Spruce Grouse	*Falcipennis canadensis*	Aves/Galliformes/Phasianidae	MAR BRD
Willow Ptarmigan	*Lagopus lagopus*	Aves/Galliformes/Phasianidae	BRD
Rock Ptarmigan	*Lagopus mutus*	Aves/Galliformes/Phasianidae	BRD
White-tailed Ptarmigan	*Lagopus leucurus*	Aves/Galliformes/Phasianidae	MAR BRD
Sandhill Crane	*Grus canadensis*	Aves/Gruiiformes/Gruidae	BRD
American Golden-Plover	*Pluvialis dominica*	Aves/Charadriiformes/Charadriidae	BRD
Pacific Golden-Plover	*Pluvialis fulva*	Aves/Charadriiformes/Charadriidae	BRD
Semipalmated Plover	*Charadrius semipalmatus*	Aves/Charadriiformes/Charadriidae	BRD
Black Oystercatcher	*Haematopus bachmani*	Aves/Charadriiformes/Haematopodidae	BRD/RES
Greater Yellowlegs	*Tringa melanoleuca*	Aves/Charadriiformes/Scolopacidae	BRD
Lesser Yellowlegs	*Tringa flavipes*	Aves/Charadriiformes/Scolopacidae	MAR BRD
Spotted Sandpiper	*Actitis macularia*	Aves/Charadriiformes/Scolopacidae	BRD
Whimbrel	*Numenius phaeopus*	Aves/Charadriiformes/Scolopacidae	BRD

Common Name	Scientific Name	Class/Order/Family	Type/Residence
Marbled Godwit	Limosa fedoa	Aves/Charadriiformes/Scolopacidae	BRD
Black Turnstone	Arenaria melanocephala	Aves/Charadriiformes/Scolopacidae	BRD
Surfbird	Aphriza virgata	Aves/Charadriiformes/Scolopacidae	BRD
Semipalmated Sandpiper	Calidris pusilla	Aves/Charadriiformes/Scolopacidae	BRD
Western Sandpiper	Calidris mauri	Aves/Charadriiformes/Scolopacidae	BRD
Least Sandpiper	Calidris minutilla	Aves/Charadriiformes/Scolopacidae	BRD
Rock Sandpiper	Calidris ptilocnemis	Aves/Charadriiformes/Scolopacidae	BRD
Dunlin	Calidris alpina	Aves/Charadriiformes/Scolopacidae	BRD
Short-billed Dowitcher	Limnodromus griseus	Aves/Charadriiformes/Scolopacidae	BRD
Common Snipe	Gallinago gallinago	Aves/Charadriiformes/Scolopacidae	BRD
Red-necked Phalarope	Phalaropus lobatus	Aves/Charadriiformes/Scolopacidae	BRD
Parasitic Jaeger	Stercorarius parasiticus	Aves/Charadriiformes/Laridae	BRD
Long-tailed Jaeger	Stercorarius longicaudus	Aves/Charadriiformes/Laridae	BRD
Bonaparte's Gull	Larus philadelphia	Aves/Charadriiformes/Laridae	BRD
Mew Gull	Larus canus	Aves/Charadriiformes/Laridae	BRD
Glaucous-winged Gull	Larus glaucescens	Aves/Charadriiformes/Laridae	BRD
Black-legged Kittiwake	Rissa tridactyla	Aves/Charadriiformes/Laridae	BRD
Arctic Tern	Sterna paradisaea	Aves/Charadriiformes/Laridae	BRD
Aleutian Tern	Sterna aleutica	Aves/Charadriiformes/Laridae	BRD
Common Murre	Uria aalge	Aves/Charadriiformes/Alcidae	BRD
Thick-billed Murre	Uria lomvia	Aves/Charadriiformes/Alcidae	BRD
Pigeon Guillemot	Cepphus columba	Aves/Charadriiformes/Alcidae	BRD
Marbled Murrelet	Brachyramphus marmoratus	Aves/Charadriiformes/Alcidae	BRD
Kittlitz's Murrelet	Brachyramphus brevirostris	Aves/Charadriiformes/Alcidae	BRD
Horned Puffin	Fratercula corniculata	Aves/Charadriiformes/Alcidae	BRD
Tufted Puffin	Fratercula cirrhata	Aves/Charadriiformes/Alcidae	BRD
Great Horned Owl	Bubo virginianus	Aves/Strigiformes/Strigidae	BRD/RES
Northern Hawk Owl	Surnia ulula	Aves/Strigiformes/Strigidae	MAR BRD
Short-eared Owl	Asio flammeus	Aves/Strigiformes/Strigidae	BRD/RES
Boreal Owl	Aegolius funereus	Aves/Strigiformes/Strigidae	MAR BRD
Northern Saw-whet Owl	Aegolius acadicus	Aves/Strigiformes/Strigidae	BRD/RES
Belted Kingfisher	Ceryle alcyon	Aves/Coraciiformes/Alcedinidae	BRD
Downy Woodpecker	Picoides pubescens	Aves/Piciformes/Picidae	BRD
Three-toed Woodpecker	Picoides tridactylus	Aves/Piciformes/Picidae	MAR BRD

Common Name	Scientific Name	Class/Order/Family	Type/Residence
Black-backed Woodpecker	Picoides arcticus	Aves/Piciformes/Picidae	MAR BRD
Northern Flicker	Colaptes auratus	Aves/Piciformes/Picidae	MAR BRD
Olive-sided Flycatcher	Contopus cooperi	Aves/Passeriformes/Tyrannidae	MAR BRD
Alder Flycatcher	Empidonax alnorum	Aves/Passeriformes/Tyrannidae	BRD
Northern Shrike	Lanius excubitor	Aves/Passeriformes/Laniidae	BRD
Gray Jay	Perisoreus canadensis	Aves/Passeriformes/Corvidae	MAR BRD
Black-billed Magpie	Pica hudsonia	Aves/Passeriformes/Corvidae	BRD/RES
Common Raven	Corvus corax	Aves/Passeriformes/Corvidae	BRD/RES
Horned Lark	Eremophila alpestris	Aves/Passeriformes/Alaudidae	BRD
Tree Swallow	Tachycineta bicolor	Aves/Passeriformes/Hirundinidae	BRD
Violet-green Swallow	Tachycineta thalassina	Aves/Passeriformes/Hirundinidae	BRD
Bank Swallow	Riparia riparia	Aves/Passeriformes/Hirundinidae	BRD
Black-capped Chickadee	Poecile atricapilla	Aves/Passeriformes/Paridae	BRD
Boreal Chickadee	Poecile hudsonica	Aves/Passeriformes/Paridae	MAR BRD
Red-breasted Nuthatch	Sitta canadensis	Aves/Passeriformes/Sittidae	MAR BRD
Brown Creeper	Certhia americana	Aves/Passeriformes/Certhiidae	MAR BRD
Winter Wren	Troglodytes troglodytes	Aves/Passeriformes/Troglodytidae	BRD
American Dipper	Cinclus mexicanus	Aves/Passeriformes/Cinclidae	BRD
Ruby-crowned Kinglet	Regulus calendula	Aves/Passeriformes/Regulidae	MAR BRD
Gray-cheeked Thrush	Catharus minimus	Aves/Passeriformes/Turdidae	BRD
Hermit Thrush	Catharus guttatus	Aves/Passeriformes/Turdidae	BRD
American Robin	Turdus migratorius	Aves/Passeriformes/Turdidae	BRD
Varied Thrush	Ixoreus naevius	Aves/Passeriformes/Turdidae	MAR BRD/MIG
American Pipit	Anthus rubescens	Aves/Passeriformes/Motacillidae	BRD
Orange-crowned Warbler	Vermivora celata	Aves/Passeriformes/Parulidae	BRD
Yellow Warbler	Dendroica petechia	Aves/Passeriformes/Parulidae	BRD
Yellow-rumped Warbler	Dendroica coronata	Aves/Passeriformes/Parulidae	MAR BRD
Blackpoll Warbler	Dendroica striata	Aves/Passeriformes/Parulidae	MAR BRD
Northern Waterthrush	Seiurus noveboracensis	Aves/Passeriformes/Parulidae	BRD
Wilson's Warbler	Wilsonia pusilla	Aves/Passeriformes/Parulidae	BRD
American Tree Sparrow	Spizella arborea	Aves/Passeriformes/Emberizidae	BRD
Savannah Sparrow	Passerculus sandwichensis	Aves/Passeriformes/Emberizidae	BRD
Fox Sparrow	Passerella iliaca	Aves/Passeriformes/Emberizidae	BRD
Song Sparrow	Melospiza melodia	Aves/Passeriformes/Emberizidae	BRD
Lincoln's Sparrow	Melospiza lincolnii	Aves/Passeriformes/Emberizidae	MAR BRD
White-crowned Sparrow	Zonotrichia leucophrys	Aves/Passeriformes/Emberizidae	BRD

Common Name	Scientific Name	Class/Order/Family	Type/Residence
Golden-crowned Sparrow	Zonotrichia atricapilla	Aves/Passeriformes/Emberizidae	BRD
Dark-eyed Junco	Junco hyemalis	Aves/Passeriformes/Emberizidae	MAR BRD
Lapland Longspur	Calcarius lapponicus	Aves/Passeriformes/Emberizidae	BRD
Snow Bunting	Plectrophenax nivalis	Aves/Passeriformes/Emberizidae	BRD
Rusty Blackbird	Euphagus carolinus	Aves/Passeriformes/Icteridae	BRD
Gray-crowned Rosy-Finch	Leucosticte tephrocotis	Aves/Passeriformes/Fringillidae	BRD
Pine Grosbeak	Pinicola enucleator	Aves/Passeriformes/Fringillidae	BRD
White-winged Crossbill	Loxia leucoptera	Aves/Passeriformes/Fringillidae	MAR BRD
Common Redpoll	Carduelis flammea	Aves/Passeriformes/Fringillidae	BRD
Pine Siskin	Carduelis pinus	Aves/Passeriformes/Fringillidae	MAR BRD

BIRDS—MIGRANT/WINTER

49 TOTAL

Common Name	Scientific Name	Class/Order/Family	Type/Residence
Yellow-billed Loon	Gavia adamsii	Aves/Gaviiformes/Gaviidae	MIG
Red-necked Grebe	Podiceps grisegena	Aves/Podicipediformes/Podicipedidae	WTR/BRD?
Sooty Shearwater	Puffinus griseus	Aves/Procellariiformes/Procellariidae	MIG/NSHR
Short-tailed Shearwater	Puffinus tenuirostris	Aves/Procellariiformes/Procellariidae	MIG/NSHR
Fork-tailed Storm-Petrel	Oceanodroma furcata	Aves/Procellariiformes/Hydrobatidae	MIG/NSHR
Leach's Storm-Petrel	Oceanodroma leucorhoa	Aves/Procellariiformes/Hydrobatidae	MIG/NSHR
Emperor Goose	Chen canagica	Aves/Anseriformes/Anatidae	MIG/NSHR
Snow Goose	Chen caerulescens	Aves/Anseriformes/Anatidae	MIG
Canada Goose	Branta canadensis	Aves/Anseriformes/Anatidae	MIG
Brant	Branta bernicla	Aves/Anseriformes/Anatidae	MIG
Eurasian Wigeon	Anas penelope	Aves/Anseriformes/Anatidae	MIG
Canvasback	Aythya valisineria	Aves/Anseriformes/Anatidae	MIG
Redhead	Aythya americana	Aves/Anseriformes/Anatidae	MIG
Ring-necked Duck	Aythya collaris	Aves/Anseriformes/Anatidae	MIG
Lesser Scaup	Aythya affinis	Aves/Anseriformes/Anatidae	MIG
Steller's Eider	Polysticta stelleri	Aves/Anseriformes/Anatidae	MIG/WTR
King Eider	Somateria spectabilis	Aves/Anseriformes/Anatidae	MIG/WTR
Surf Scoter	Melanitta perspicillata	Aves/Anseriformes/Anatidae	MIG/WTR
White-winged Scoter	Melanitta fusca	Aves/Anseriformes/Anatidae	MIG/WTR
Long-tailed Duck	Clangula hyemalis	Aves/Anseriformes/Anatidae	MIG/WTR
Bufflehead	Bucephala albeola	Aves/Anseriformes/Anatidae	WTR/BRD?
Barrow's Goldeneye	Bucephala islandica	Aves/Anseriformes/Anatidae	MIG

Common Name	Scientific Name	Class/Order/Family	Type/Residence
Sharp-shinned Hawk	*Accipiter striatus*	Aves/Falconiformes/Accipitridae	MIG
Black-bellied Plover	*Pluvialis squatarola*	Aves/Charadriiformes/Charadriidae	MIG
Solitary Sandpiper	*Tringa solitaria*	Aves/Charadriiformes/Scolopacidae	MIG/BRD?
Wandering Tattler	*Heteroscelus incanus*	Aves/Charadriiformes/Scolopacidae	MIG
Bristle-thighed Curlew	*Numenius tahitiensis*	Aves/Charadriiformes/Scolopacidae	MIG
Bar-tailed Godwit	*Limosa lapponica*	Aves/Charadriiformes/Scolopacidae	MIG
Ruddy Turnstone	*Arenaria interpres*	Aves/Charadriiformes/Scolopacidae	MIG
Red Knot	*Calidris canutus*	Aves/Charadriiformes/Scolopacidae	MIG
Sanderling	*Calidris alba*	Aves/Charadriiformes/Scolopacidae	MIG
Baird's Sandpiper	*Calidris bairdii*	Aves/Charadriiformes/Scolopacidae	MIG
Pectoral Sandpiper	*Calidris melanotos*	Aves/Charadriiformes/Scolopacidae	MIG
Sharp-tailed Sandpiper	*Calidris acuminata*	Aves/Charadriiformes/Scolopacidae	MIG
Stilt Sandpiper	*Calidris himantopus*	Aves/Charadriiformes/Scolopacidae	MIG
Buff-breasted Sandpiper	*Tryngites subruficollis*	Aves/Charadriiformes/Scolopacidae	MIG
Long-billed Dowitcher	*Limnodromus scolopaceus*	Aves/Charadriiformes/Scolopacidae	MIG
Red Phalarope	*Phalaropus fulicaria*	Aves/Charadriiformes/Scolopacidae	MIG
Pomarine Jaeger	*Stercorarius pomarinus*	Aves/Charadriiformes/Laridae	MIG
Herring Gull	*Larus argentatus*	Aves/Charadriiformes/Laridae	MIG
Glaucous Gull	*Larus hyperboreus*	Aves/Charadriiformes/Laridae	MIG/WTR
Snowy Owl	*Nyctea scandiaca*	Aves/Strigiformes/Strigidae	WIN/TRAN
Say's Phoebe	*Sayornis saya*	Aves/Passeriformes/Tyrannidae	MIG/BRD?
Golden-crowned Kinglet	*Regulus satrapa*	Aves/Passeriformes/Regulidae	MIG
Swainson's Thrush	*Catharus ustulatus*	Aves/Passeriformes/Turdidae	MIG
Townsend's Warbler	*Dendroica townsendi*	Aves/Passeriformes/Parulidae	MIG
Chipping Sparrow	*Spizella passerina*	Aves/Passeriformes/Emberizidae	MIG
McKay's Bunting	*Plectrophenax hyperboreus*	Aves/Passeriformes/Emberizidae	MIG/WTR
Hoary Redpoll	*Carduelis hornemanni*	Aves/Passeriformes/Fringillidae	MIG/WTR
POSSIBLE BREEDERS		6 TOTAL	
Hudsonian Godwit	*Limosa haemastica*	Aves/Charadriiformes/Scolopacidae	BRD?
Cliff Swallow	*Petrochelidon pyrrhonota*	Aves/Passeriformes/Hirundinidae	BRD?
Barn Swallow	*Hirundo rustica*	Aves/Passeriformes/Hirundinidae	BRD?
Yellow Wagtail	*Motacilla flava*	Aves/Passeriformes/Motacillidae	BRD?
Northwestern Crow	*Corvus caurinus*	Aves/Passeriformes/Corvidae	BRD?

Common Name	Scientific Name	Class/Order/Family	Type/Residence
Horned Grebe	*Podiceps auritus*	Aves/Podicipediformes/Podicipedidae	BRD?
BIRDS—EXOTIC		2 TOTAL	
Rock Dove	*Columba livia*	Aves/Columbiiformes/Columbidae	Exotic
European Starling	*Sturnus vulgaris*	Aves/Passeriformes/Sturnidae	Exotic
BIRDS— TRANSIENT/CONFIRMED		10 TOTAL	
Red-tailed Hawk	*Buteo jamaicensis*	Aves/Falconiformes/Accipitridae	TRAN
American Kestrel	*Falco sparverius*	Aves/Falconiformes/Falconidae	TRAN
Slaty-backed Gull	*Larus schistisagus*	Aves/Charadriiformes/Laridae	TRAN
Sabine's Gull	*Xema sabini*	Aves/Charadriiformes/Laridae	TRAN
Rufous Hummingbird	*Selasphorus rufus*	Aves/Apodiformes/Trochilidae	TRAN
Hairy Woodpecker	*Picoides villosus*	Aves/Piciformes/Picidae	TRAN
Western Wood-Pewee	*Contopus sordidulus*	Aves/Passeriformes/Tyrannidae	TRAN
Steller's Jay	*Cyanocitta stelleri*	Aves/Passeriformes/Corvidae	TRAN
Townsend's Solitaire	*Myadestes townsendi*	Aves/Passeriformes/Turdidae	TRAN
Tennessee Warbler	*Vermivora peregrina*	Aves/Passeriformes/Parulidae	TRAN
BIRDS— ACCIDENTAL/CONFIRMED		12 TOTAL	
Great Egret	*Ardea alba*	Aves/Ciconiiformes/Ardeidae	ACC
Bean Goose	*Anser fabalis*	Aves/Anseriformes/Anatidae	ACC
Garganey	*Anas querquedula*	Aves/Anseriformes/Anatidae	ACC
Baikal Teal	*Anas formosa*	Aves/Anseriformes/Anatidae	ACC
Tufted Duck	*Aythya fuligula*	Aves/Anseriformes/Anatidae	ACC
Common Greenshank	*Tringa nebularia*	Aves/Charadriiformes/Scolopacidae	ACC
Black-headed Gull	*Larus ridibundus*	Aves/Charadriiformes/Laridae	ACC
Ring-billed Gull	*Larus delawarensis*	Aves/Charadriiformes/Laridae	ACC
Sky Lark	*Alauda arvensis*	Aves/Passeriformes/Alaudidae	ACC
Olive-backed Pipit	*Anthus hodgsoni*	Aves/Passeriformes/Motacillidae	ACC
Bohemian Waxwing	*Bombycilla garrulus*	Aves/Passeriformes/Bombacillidae	ACC
Brown-headed Cowbird	*Molothrus ater*	Aves/Passeriformes/Icteridae	ACC

Common Name	Scientific Name	Class/Order/Family	Type/Residence
BIRDS-NEARSHORE		9-TOTAL	
Northern Fulmar	Fulmarus glacialis	Aves/Procellariiformes/Procellariidae	NSHR
Spectacled Eider	Somateria fischeri	Aves/Anseriformes/Anatidae	NSHR
Ancient Murrelet	Synthliboramphus antiquus	Aves/Charadriiformes/Alcidae	NSHR
Cassin's Auklet	Ptychoramphus aleuticus	Aves/Charadriiformes/Alcidae	NSHR
Parakeet Auklet	Aethia psittacula	Aves/Charadriiformes/Alcidae	NSHR
Least Auklet	Aethia pusilla	Aves/Charadriiformes/Alcidae	NSHR
Whiskered Auklet	Aethia pygmaea	Aves/Charadriiformes/Alcidae	NSHR
Crested Auklet	Aethia cristatella	Aves/Charadriiformes/Alcidae	NSHR
Rhinoceros Auklet	Cerorhinca monocerata	Aves/Charadriiformes/Alcidae	NSHR
MAMMALS-TERRESTRIAL			
Montane (Dusky) Shrew	Sorex monticolus	Mammalia/Insectivora/Scoricidae	RES
Cinereus (Masked) Shrew	Sorex cinereus	Mammalia/Insectivora/Scoricidae	RES
Tundra Shrew	Sorex tundrensis	Mammalia/Insectivora/Scoricidae	RES
Little Brown Bat	Myotis lucifugas	Mammalia/Chiroptera/Vespertilionidae	MAR BRD?
Coyote	Canis latrans	Mammalia/Carnivora/Canidae	RES
Gray Wolf	Canis lupus	Mammalia/Carnivora/Canidae	RES
Red Fox	Vulpes vulpes	Mammalia/Carnivora/Canidae	RES
Brown Bear	Ursus arctos	Mammalia/Carnivora/Ursidae	RES
Short-tailed Weasel	Mustela erminea	Mammalia/Carnivora/Mustelidae	RES
Least Weasel	Mustela nivalis	Mammalia/Carnivora/Mustelidae	RES
Mink	Mustela vison	Mammalia/Carnivora/Mustelidae	RES
Wolverine	Gulo gulo	Mammalia/Carnivora/Mustelidae	RES
River Otter	Lontra canadensis	Mammalia/Carnivora/Mustelidae	RES
Lynx	Lynx Canadensis	Mammalia/Carnivora/Felidae	RES
Moose	Alces alces	Mammalia/Artiodactyla/Cervidae	RES
Caribou	Rangifer tarandus	Mammalia/Artiodactyla/Cervidae	RES
Hoary Marmot	Marmota caligata	Mammalia/Rodentia/Sciuridae	RES
Arctic Ground Squirrel	Spermophilus parryii (undulatus)	Mammalia/Rodentia/Sciuridae	RES

Common Name	Scientific Name	Class/Order/Family	Type/Residence
Red Squirrel	*Tamiasciurus Hudsonicus*	Mammalia/Rodentia/Sciuridae	MAR RES?
Beaver	*Castor canadesis*	Mammalia/Rodentia/Castoridae	RES
Red-backed Vole	*Cletherionomys rutilus*	Mammalia/Rodentia/Muridae	RES
Tundra Vole	*Microtus oeconomus*	Mammalia/Rodentia/Muridae	RES
Meadow Vole?	*Microtus pennsylvanicus*	Mammalia/Rodentia/Muridae	MAR RES?
Muskrat?	*Ondatra zibethicus*	Mammalia/Rodentia/Muridae	MAR RES?
Brown Lemming	*Lemmus sibiricus*	Mammalia/Rodentia/Muridae	RES
Northern Bog Lemming	*Synaptomys borealis*	Mammalia/Rodentia/Muridae	RES
Northern (Collared) Lemming	*Dicrostonyx groeniandicus*	Mammalia/Rodentia/Muridae	RES
Meadow Jumping Mouse	*Zapus hudsonius*	Mammalia/Rodentia/Dipodidae	RES
Porcupine	*Erethizon dorsatum*	Mammalia/Rodentia/Erethizontidae	RES
Snowshoe (Varying) Hare	*Lepus americanus*	Mammalia/Lagomorpha/Leporidae	RES
Alaskan (Tundra) Hare	*Lepus othus*	Mammalia/Lagomorpha/Leporidae	RES
MAMMALS—MARINE			
Sea Otter	*Enhydra lutris*	Mammalia/Carnivora/Mustelidae	RES
Steller Sea-lion	*Eumetopias jubatus*	Mammalia/Carnivora/Otariidae	RES
Harbor Seal	*Phoca vitulina*	Mammalia/Carnivora/Phocidae	RES
ACC or NEARSHORE MARINE MAMMALS[4]			
Walrus	*Odobenus resmorus*	Mammalia/Carnivora/Odobenidae	NSRH
Northern Fur Seal	*Callorhinus ursinus*	Mammalia/Carnivora/Otariidae	TRAN
N. Right Whale	*Eubalaena glacialis*	Mammalia/Cetacea/Balaenidae	NSHR
Minke Whale	*Balaenoptera acutorostrata*	Mammalia/Cetacea/Balaenopteridae	NSHR
Humpback Whale	*Megaptera novaeangliae*	Mammalia/Cetacea/Balaenopteridae	NSHR
Gray Whale	*Eschrichtius robustus*	Mammalia/Cetacea/Eschrichtidae	NSHR
Pacific White-sided Dolphin	*Lagenorhynchus obliquidens*	Mammalia/Cetacea/Delphinidae	NSHR

---

[4] Of the species listed in this section, only Gray Whales and Orcas have been documented within Refuge boundaries. While the other species have not been documented within Refuge boundaries, they are present in nearshore areas.

Alaska Peninsula and Becharof National Wildlife Refuges

Common Name	Scientific Name	Class/Order/Family	Type/Residence
Pilot Whale	*Globicephala sp*	Mammalia/Cetacea/Delphinidae	NSHR
Killer Whale	*Orcinus Orca*	Mammalia/Cetacea/Delphinidae	NSHR
Beluga	*Delphinapterus leucas*	Mammalia/Cetacea/Monodentidae	NSHR on BB side
Harbor Porpoise	*Phocoena phocoena*	Mammalia/Cetacea/Phocoenidae	NSHR
Dall Porpoise	*Phocoenoides dalli*	Mammalia/Cetacea/Phocoenidae	NSHR

Common Name	Scientific Name (family, species) (DOI 1974)
Club Moss Family	LYCOPODIACEAE
Fir Club Moss	*Lycopodium selago*
Stiff Club Moss	*Lycopodium annotinum*
Common Club Moss	*Lycopodium clavatum*
Alpine Club Moss	*Lycopodium alpinum*
Quiltwort Family	ISOETACFAE
	Isoetes muricata
Horsetail Family	EQUISETACEAE
	Equisetum fluviatile
	Equisetum silvaticum
	Equisetum arvense
Adder's Tongue Family	OPHIOGLOSSACEAE
Moonwort	*Botrychium lunaria*
	Botrychium lanceolatum
Mountain Parsley Family	CRYPTOGRAMMACEAE
Parsley Fern	*Cryptogramma crispa*
Marsh Fern Family	THEYPTERIDACEAE
	Thelypteris phegopteris
Lady Fern Family	ATHYRIACEAE
Lady Fern	*Athyrium filix-femina*
Fragile Fern	*Cystopteris fragilis*
Shield Fern Family	ASPIDIACEAE
	Dryopteris dilatata
	Gymnocarpium dryopteris
Licorice Fern Family	POLYPODIACEAE
	Polypodium vulgare
Bur Reed Family	SPARGANIACEAE
	Sparganium hyperboreum
Pondweed Family	POTAMOGETONACEAE
Eelgrass	*Zostera marina*
	Potamogeton alpinus
	Potamogeton perfoliatus
	Potamogeton filiformis
Ditch Grass	*Ruppia spiralis*
Arrow Grass Family	JUNCAGINACEAE
	Trigolochin maritimum
	Trigolochin palustris
Grass Family	GRAMINEAE
Holy Grass	*Hierochloe alpina*
Vanilla grass	*Hierochloe odorata*
Mountain Timothy	*Phleum commutatum*
Timothy	*Phleum pratense*

Common Name	Scientific Name (family, species) (DOI 1974)
Foxtail	*Alopecurus aequalis*
Polar Grass	*Arctagr stis latifolia*
Wood Reed Grass	*Cinna latifolia*
Bent Grass	*Agrostis alaskana*
	Agrostis exarata
	Agrostis seabra
	Agrostis geminata
Bluejoint	*Calamogrostis canadensis*
	Deschampsia caespitosa
	Deschampsia beringensis
	Vahlodea atropurpurea
	Trisetum spicatum
	Poa arctica
	Poa eminens
	Poa palustris
	Poa nemoralis
	Poa hispidula
	Poa stenantha
	Poa annua
	Poa brachyanthera
Alkali Grass	*Puccinellia nutkaensis*
Fuscue Grass	*Festuca altaica*
	Festuca rubra
Brome Grass	*Bromus ciliatus*
	Hordeum brach
	Yantherum
Lyme Grass	*Elymus arenarius*
Sedge Family	CYPERACEAE
Cotton Grass	*Eriophorum angustifolium*
	Eriophorum russeolum
	Trichophorum caespitosum
Sedge	*Carex anthoxanthea*
	Carex circinnata
	Carex nigricans
	Carex macrocephala
	Carex macloviana
	Carex canescens
	Carex Kelloggii
	Carex aquatlilis
	Carex Lyngbyaei
	Carex stylosa
	Carex Gmelini
	Carex machrochaeta
	Carex spectabilis
	Carex nesophila
	Carex pluriflora
	Carex saxatilis
Rush Family	JUNCACEAE
	Juncus arcticus
	Juncus mertensianus
	Juncus castaneus
Wood Rush	*Luzula wahlenbergii*

Common Name	Scientific Name (family, species) (DOI 1974)
	Luzula parviflora
	Luzula arcuata
	Luzula tundricola
	Luzula multiflora
	Luzula spicata
Lily Family	LILIACEAE
False Asphodel	*Tofieldia coccinea*
Kamchatka Fritillary, Sarana	*Fritillaria camschatcensis*
Alp Lily	*Lloydia serotina*
Twisted-stalk	*Streptopus amplexifolius*
Iris Family	IRIDACEAE
Wild Flag	*Iris setosa*
Orchid Family	ORCHIDACEAE
Lady's Slipper	*Cypripedium guttatum*
Key Flower	*Dactylorhiza aristata*
Frog Orchid	*Coeloglossum viride*
Bog Orchid	*Platanthera convallariaefoia*
Ladies' Tresses	*Platanthera dilatata*
	Spiranthes romanzoffiana
	Listera cordata
Willow Family	SALICACEAE
Balsam Poplar, Cottonwood	*Populus balsamifera*
Netted Willow	*Salix reticulata*
	Salix routundifolia
	Salix arctica
	Salix fuscescens
	Salix cyclophylla
	Salix glauca
	Salix barclayi
	Salix commutata
Alaska Willow	*Salix alaxensis*
	Salix rulchra
Birch Family	BETULCEAE
Sitka Alder	*Alnus crispa*
	Alnus sinuata
	Betula kenaica
Nettle Family	URTICACEAE
	Urtica gracilis
Buckwheat Family	POLYGONACEAE
	Koenigia islandica
Sheep Sorrel	*Rumex acetosella*
	Rumex graminifolius
	Rumex fenestratus
Mountain Sorrel	*Oxyria digyna*
	Polygonum viviparum
Mountain Sorrel	*Polygonum caurianum*
Goosefoot Family	CHENOPODIACEAE

Common Name	Scientific Name (family, species) (DOI 1974)
	Atiplex alaskensis
Pursalane Family	PORTULACEAE
Spring Beauty	*Claytonia sibrica*
	Claytonia sarmentosa
	Claytonia chamissoi
Water Blinks	*Montia fontana*
Pink Family	CARYOPHYLLACEAE
Chickweed	*Stellaria media*
	Stellaria crispa
	Stellaria humifusa
	Stellaria calycantha
	Stellaria sitchana
	Stellaria monantha
Mouse-ear Chickweed	*Cerastium berringianum*
	Cerastium fischerianum
	Cerastium fontanum
Pearlwort	*Sagina intermedia*
	Sagina crassicaulis
	Minuartia macrocarpa
	Minuartia arctica
	Minuartia rubella
	Honckenya peploides
Grove Sandwort	*Moehringia lateriflora*
Moss Campion	*Silene acaulis*
Water Lily Family	NYMPHAEACEAE
Yellow pond Lily	*Nuphar polysepalum*
Crowfoot Family	RANUNCULACEAE
	Caltha palustris
	Actaea rubra
Monkshood	*Aconitum delphinifolium*
	Aconitum maximum
	Coptis trifolia
	Anemone richardsonii
	Anemone parviflors
	Anemone narcissiflora
Buttercup, Crowfoot	*Ranunculus sp.*
White Water Crowfoot	*Ranunculus trichophyllus*
Creeping Spearwort	*Ranunculus reptans*
	Ranunculus eschscholtzii
	Ranunculus Bongardi
Meadow Rue	*Thalictrum sparsiflorum*
Poppy Family	PAPAVERACEAE
	Papaver alaskanum
Earth Smoke Family	FUMARIACEA
	Corydalis pauciflora
Mustard Family	CRUCIFERAE
Winter Cress	*Barbarea orthoceras*

Common Name	Scientific Name (family, species) (DOI 1974)
Yellow Cress	*Rorippa islandica*
Bitter Cress	*Cardamine bellidifolia*
Cuckoo Flower	*Cardamine pratensis*
	Capsella rubella
	Draba nivalis
	Draba borealis
Rock Cress	*Arabis lyrata*
	Arabis hirsuta
Sundew Family	DROSERACEA
	Drosera rotundifolia
Stonecrop Family	CRASSUIACEAE
Roseroot	*Sedum rosea*
Saxifrage Family	SAXIFRAGACEAE
Leatherleaved Saxifrage	*Leptarrhena pyrolifolia*
Purple Mountain Saxifrage	*Saxifraga oppositifolia*
	Saxifraga serpyllifolia
Box Saxifrage	*Saxifraga hirculus*
Spotted Saxifrage	*Saxifraga bronchialis*
	Saxifraga punctata
	Saxifraga bracteata
	Saxifraga rivularis
	Saxifraga unalaschcensis
Snow Saxifrage	*Saxifraga nivalis*
Coast Saxifrage	*Saxifraga ferruginea*
Tufted Saxifrage	*Saxifraga caespitosa*
Alpine Heuchera	*Heuchera glabra*
Fringe Cups	*Tellima grandiflora*
Northern Water Carpet	*Chrysosplenium tetrandrum*
	Chrysosplenium wrightii
	Parnassia kotzebuei
	Parnassia palustris
Rose Family	ROSACEAE
Alaskan Spiraea	*Spiraea beauverdiana*
	Luetkea pectinata
Goatsbeard	*Aruncus sylvester*
	Rubus arcticus
Cloudberry	*Rubus chamaemorus*
Salmonberry	*Rubus spectabilis*
Marsh Fivefinger	*Potentilla palustris*
	Potentilla villosa
Pacific Silverweed	*Potentilla Egedii*
	Sibbaldia procumbens
Avens	*Geum macrophyllum*
	Geum Rossii
Burnet	*Sanguisorba stipulata*
	Fragaria chiloensis
	Dryas sp.

Common Name	Scientific Name (family, species) (DOI 1974)
Pea Family	LEGUMINOSAE
Lupine	*Lupinus nootkatensis*
Milk Vetch	*Astragalus polaris*
	Oxtropis Maydellians
	Oxtropis nigrescens
	Lathyrus maritimus
Vetchling	*Lathyrus palustris*
Geranium Family	GERANIACEAE
	Geranium erianthum
Water Startwort Family	CALLITRICHACEA
	Callitriche verna
Violet Family	VIOLACEAE
	Viola biflora
	Viola langsdorfii
	Viola epipsila
Evening Primrose Family	ONAGRACEAE
Willow Herb	*Epilobium angustifolium*
River Beauty	*Epilobium latifolium*
	Epilobium luteum
	Epilobium palustre
	Epilobium leptocarpum
	Epilobium glandulosum
	Epilobium sertulatum
	Epilobium anagallidifolium
	Epilobi Hornemannii
Enchanter's Nightshade	*Circaea alpina*
Water Milfoil Family	HALORAGACEAE
Mare's Tail	*Hippuris vulgaris*
	Hippuris tetraphylla
Parsley Family	UMBELLIFERAE
Water Hemlock	*Cicuta mackenzieana*
Beach Lovage	*Ligusticum scoticum*
Hemlock Parsley	*Conioselinum chinese*
Wild Celery	*Angelica lucida*
Cow parsnip	*Heracleum lanatum*
	Bupleurum triradiatum
Dogwood Family	CORNACEAE
Swedish Dwarf Cornel	*Cornus suecica*
Bunchberry; Canadian DwarfCornel	*Cornus canadensis*
Wintergreen Family	PYROLACEAE
	Pyrola asarifolia
	Pyrola secunda
	Pyrola minor
Crowberry Family	EMPETRACEAE
	Empetrum nigrum.

Common Name	Scientific Name (family, species) (DOI 1974)
Heath Family	ERICACEAE
Labrador Tea	*Ledum palustre*
Kamchatka Rhododendron	*Rhododendron camtschaticum*
Alpine Azalea	*Loiseleuria procumbens*
Mountain Heather	*Phyllodoce aleutica*
Alaska Moss Heath	*Cassiope stelleriana*
	Cassiope lycopodioides
	Andromeda polifolia
	Arctostaphylos alpina
	Arctostaphylos uva-ursi
Lingonberry	*Vaccinium vitis-idaea*
Alpine Blueberry	*Vaccinium uliginosum*
	Vaccinium ovalifolium
Cranberry	*Oxycoccus microcarpus*
Diapensia Family	DIAPENSIACEAE
	Diapensia lapponica
Primrose Family	PRIMULACEAE
	Primula cuneifolia
Greenland Primrose	*Primula egaliksensis*
	Androsace chamaejasme
	Androsace alaskana
Starflower	*Trientalis europaea*
Leadwort Family	PLUMBAGINACEAE
Thrift	*Armeria maritima*
Genetian Family	GENTIANACEAE
	Gentiana algida
	Gentiana amarella
Buckbean	*Menyanthes trifoliata*
	Swertia perennis
Polemoaium Family	POLEMONIACEAE
	Polenomium acutiflorum
Borage Family	BORAGINACEAE
	Myosotis alpestris
	Mertensia maritima
Figwort Family	SCROPHULARIACEAE
	Mimulus sp.
	Veronica sp.
	Lagotis glauca
	Castilleja unalaschensis
	Rhinanthus minor
	Pedicularis kanei
	Pedicularis capitata
Bladderwort Family	LENTIBULARIACEAE
	Pinguicula vulgaris
Madder Family	RUBIACEAE
	Galeum sp.

Common Name	Scientific Name (family, species) (DOI 1974)
Honeysuckle Family	CAPRIFOLIACEAE *Sambucus racemosa* *Viburnum edula*
Valerian Family	VALERIANACEAE *Valeriana capitata*
Bluebell Family	CAMPANULACEAE *Campanula lasiocarpa*
Composite Family Goldenrod	COMPOSITAE *Solidago multiradiata* *Solidago lepida* *Aster sibiricus*
Coastal Fleabane	*Erigeron peregrinus*
Pussytoe	*Antennaria monocephala*
Pearly Everlasting	*Anaphalis argaritacea*
Yarrow	*Achillea borealis*
Pineapple Weed	*Matricaria matricatiodes*
Arctic Daisy	*Chrysanthemum arcticum*
Wormwood	*Artemisia globularia* *Artemisia tilesii* *Artemisia arctica* *Petasites frigidus* *Petasites hyperboreusS* *Arnica Lessingii* *Arnica Chamissonis*
Groundsel, Ragwort	*Senecio resedifolius* *Senecio pseudo-Arnica*
Dandelion	*Taraxacum trignolobum*
Rattlesnake Root	*Prenanthes alata*

DOI. 1974. "Proposed Katmai National Park, Alaska." Final environmental impact statement. Washington, D.C.: U.S. Department of the Interior.

7. Appendix D:
Maps

Figure 2: Becharof National Wildlife Refuge

Figure 3: Ugashik Unit, Alaska Peninsula National Wildlife Refuge

Figure 4: Chignik Unit, Alaska Peninsula National Wildlife Refuge and
Seal Cape Unit, Alaska Maritime National Wildlife Refuge

Figure 5: Yantarni Bay Moderate Management Area

Figure 6: Current Management Categories

Figure 7: Generalized Land Status

Figure 8: Native Corporation Lands

Figure 9: ANCSA Section 17(b) Easements

Figure 10: Asserted RS-2477 Routes

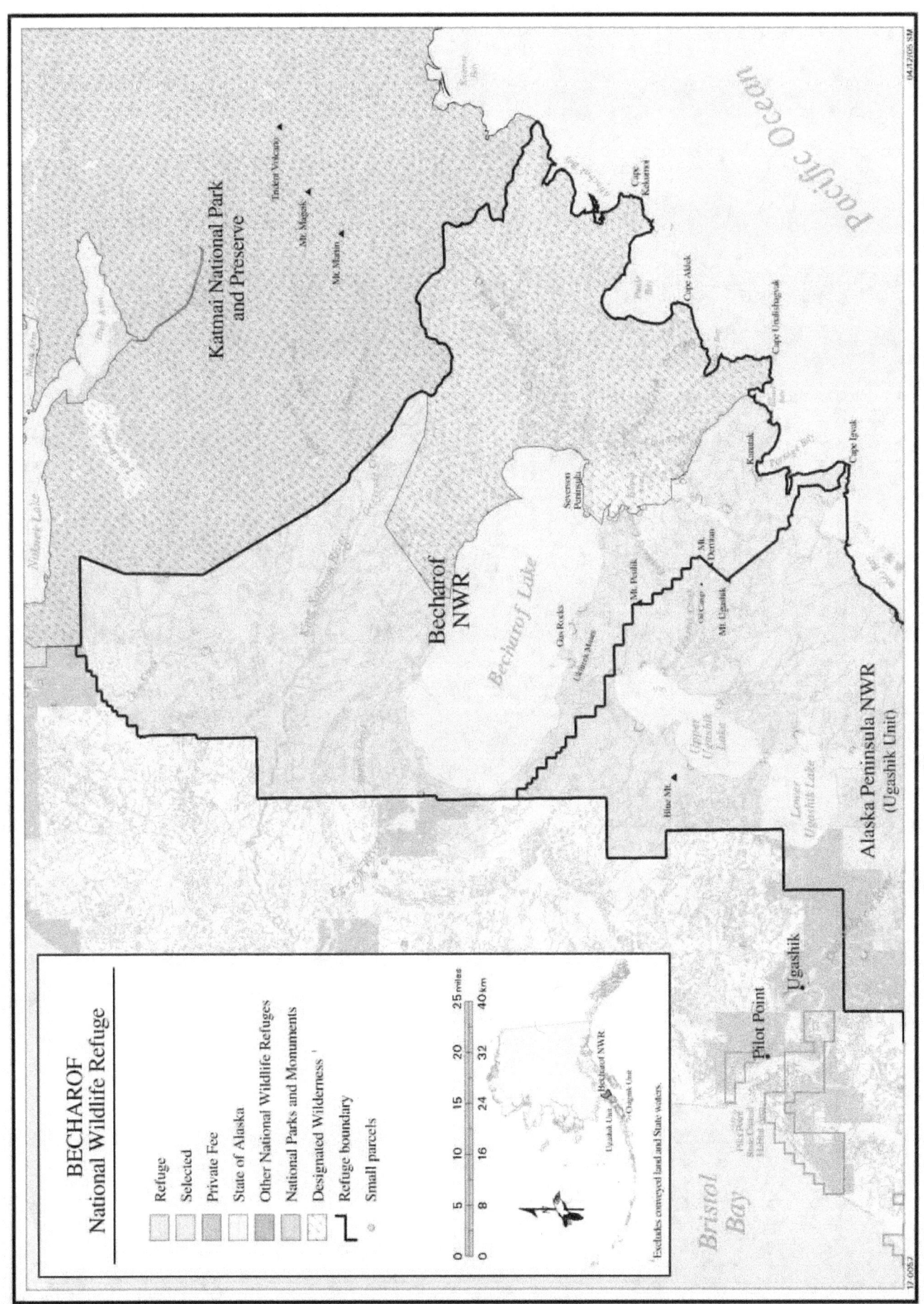

Figure 2: Becharof National Wildlife Refuge
Comprehensive Conservation Plan

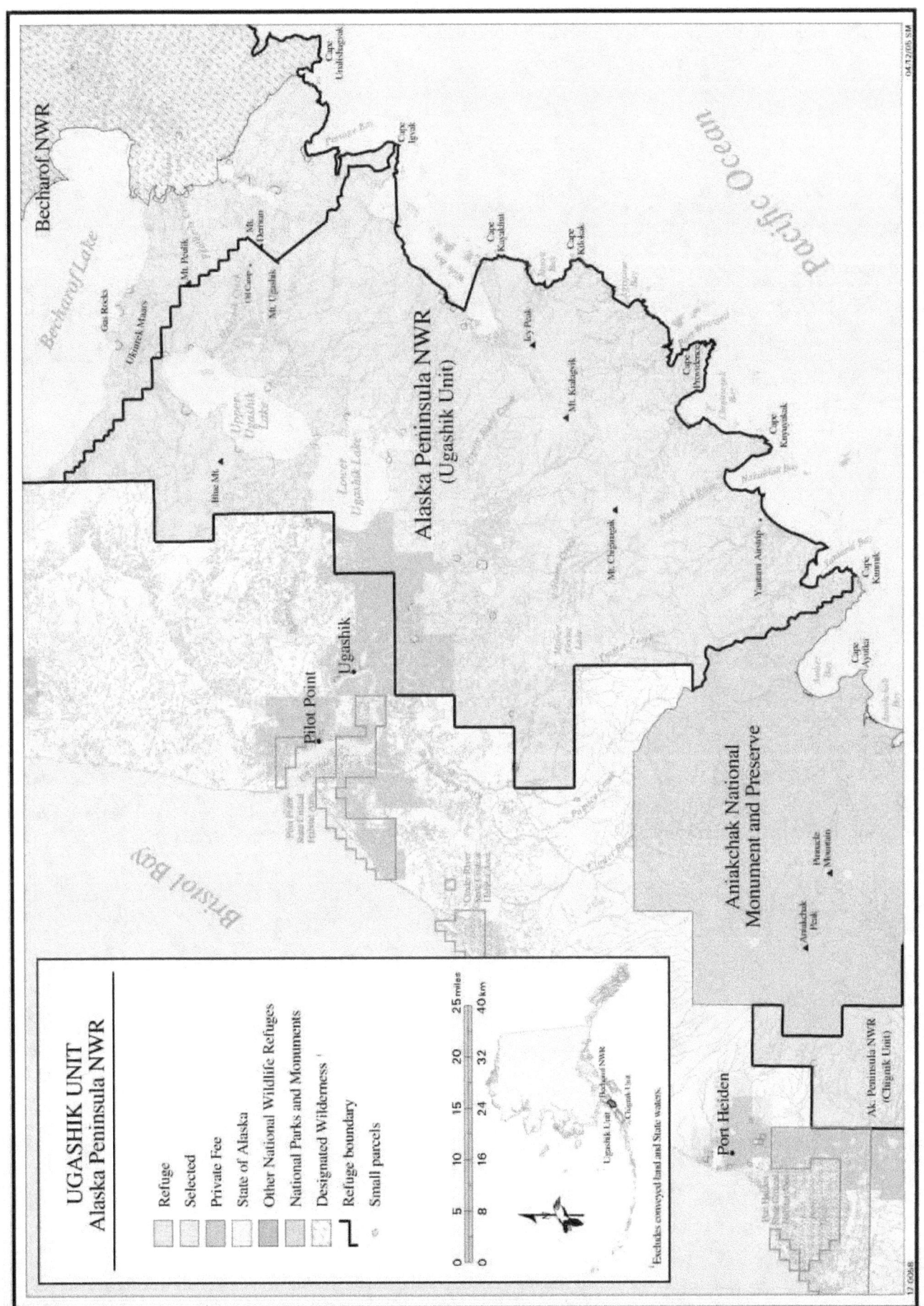

Figure 3: Ugashik Unit, Alaska Peninsula NWR
Comprehensive Conservation Plan

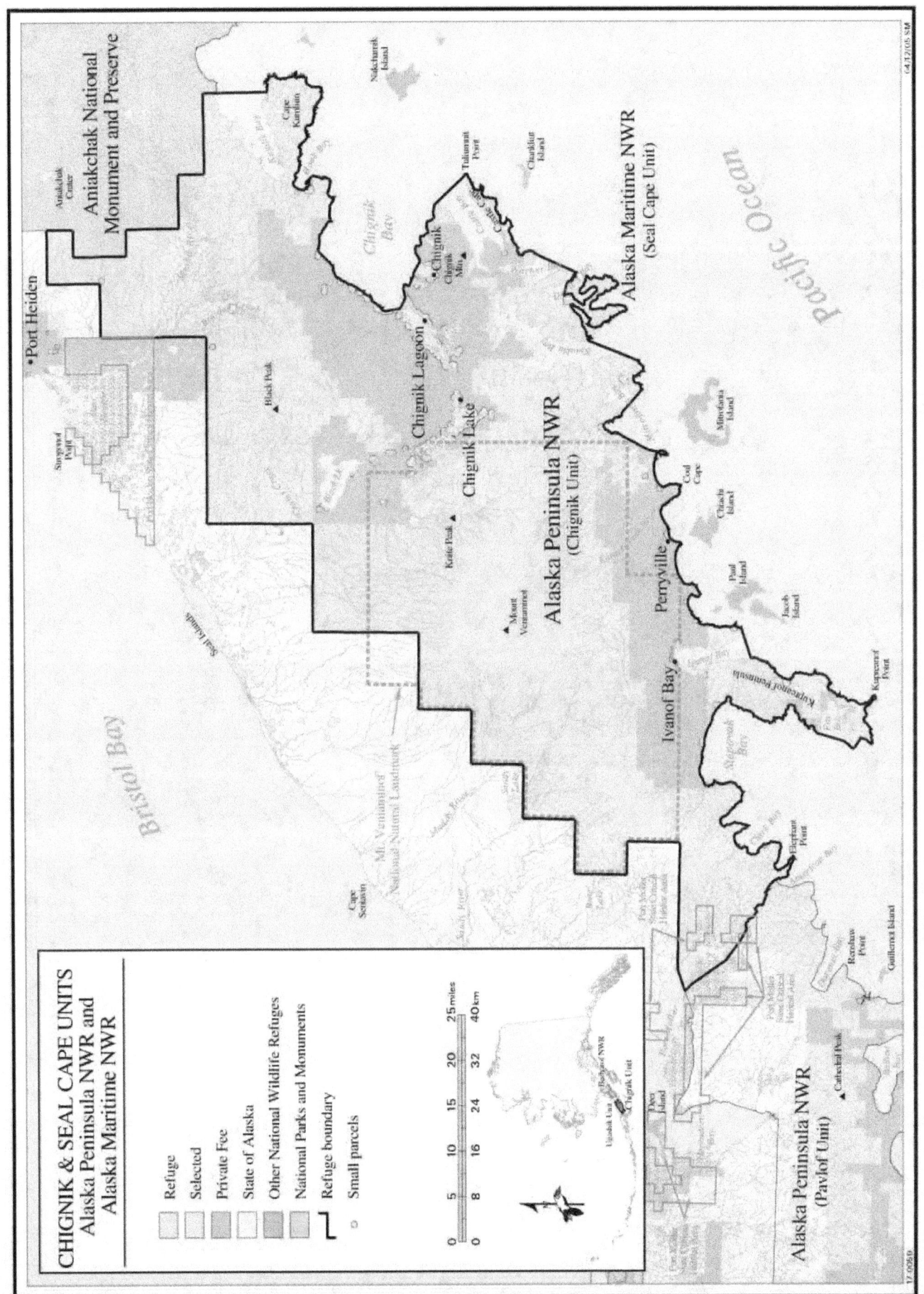

Figure 4: Chignik and Seal Cape Units
Comprehensive Conservation Plan

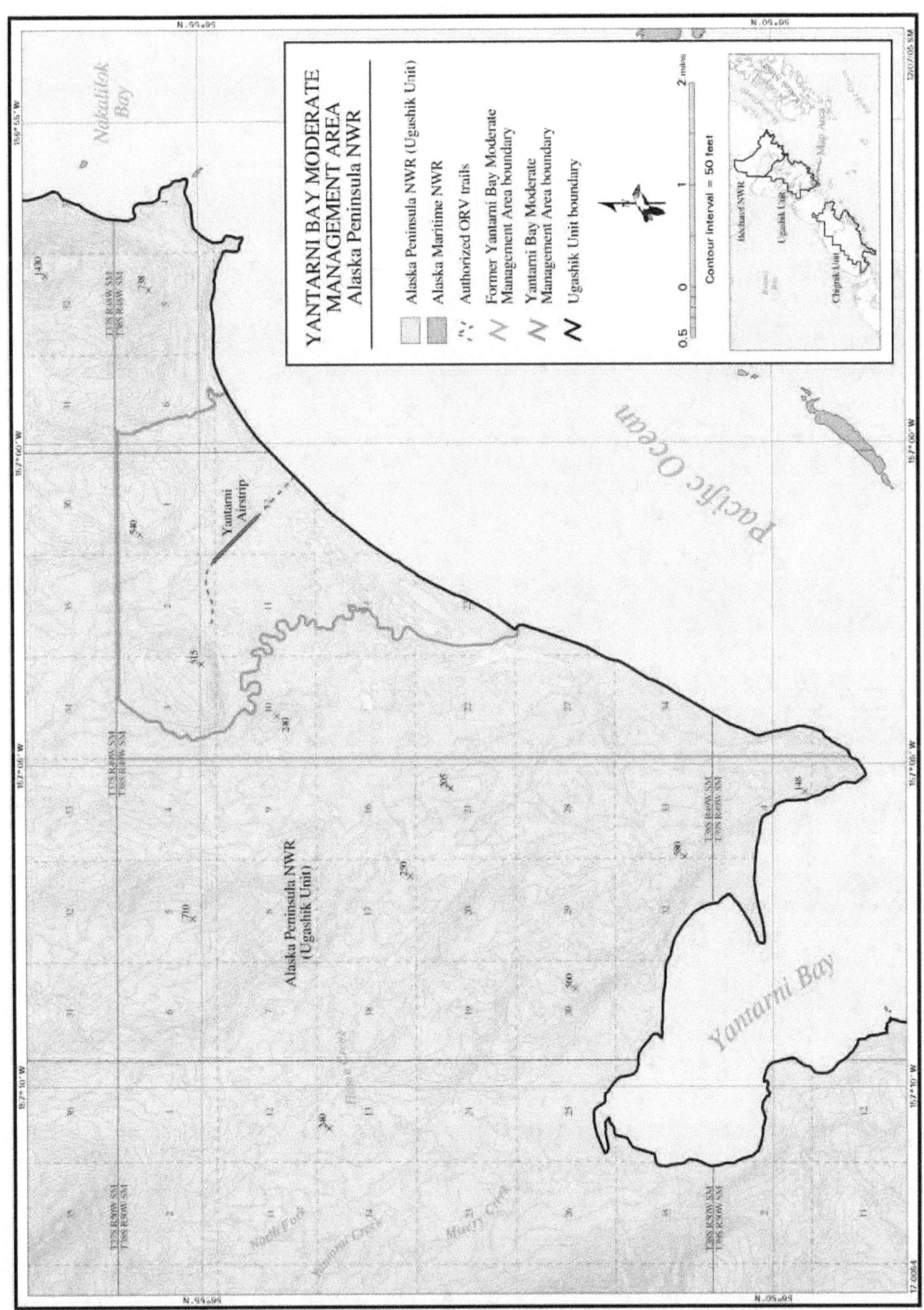

Figure 5: Yantarni Bay Moderate Management Area
Comprehensive Conservation Plan

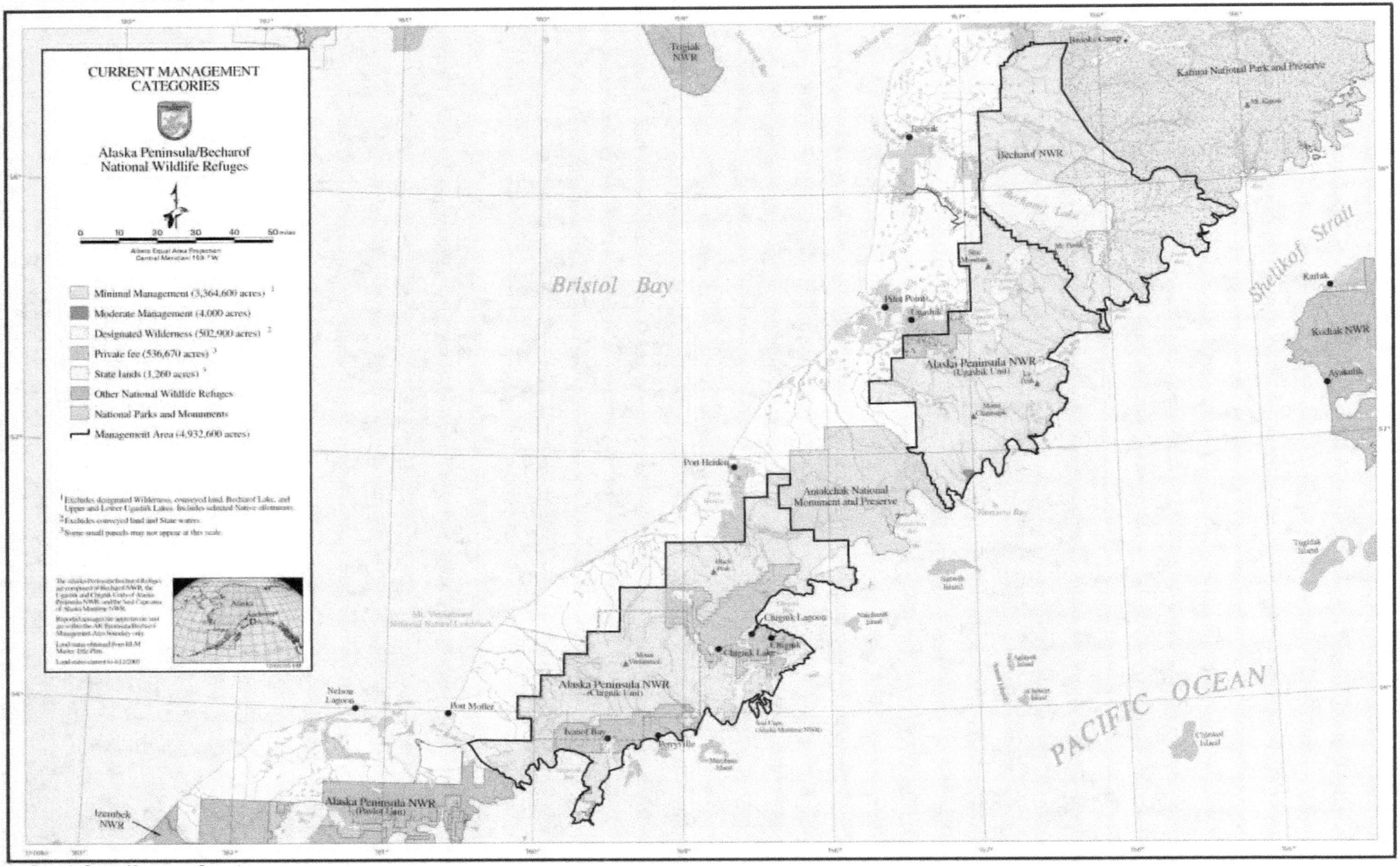

Alaska Peninsula and Becharof National Wildlife Refuges

Figure 6 Current Management Categories
Comprehensive Conservation Plan
127

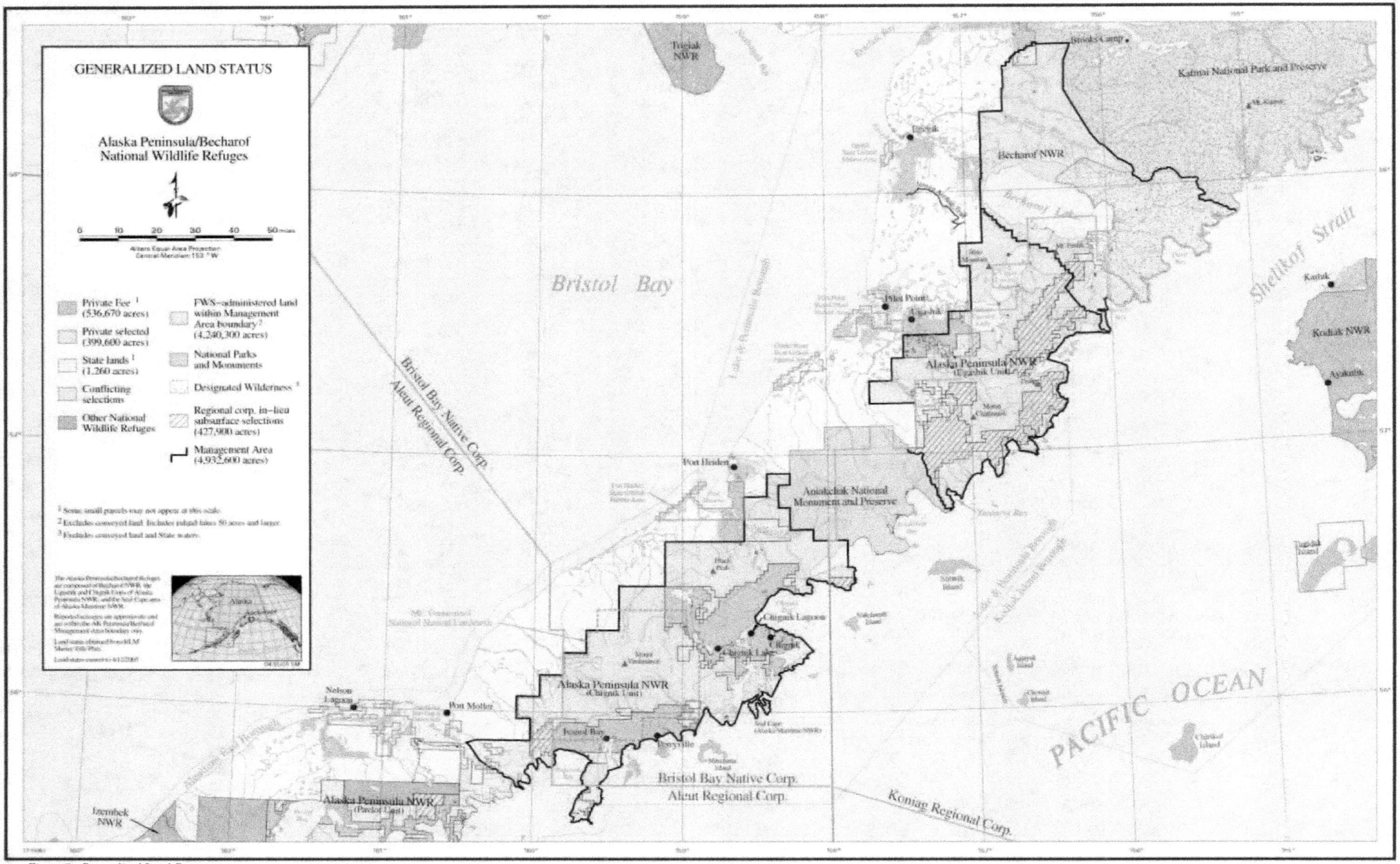

Figure 7 Generalized Land Status
Comprehensive Conservation Plan
129

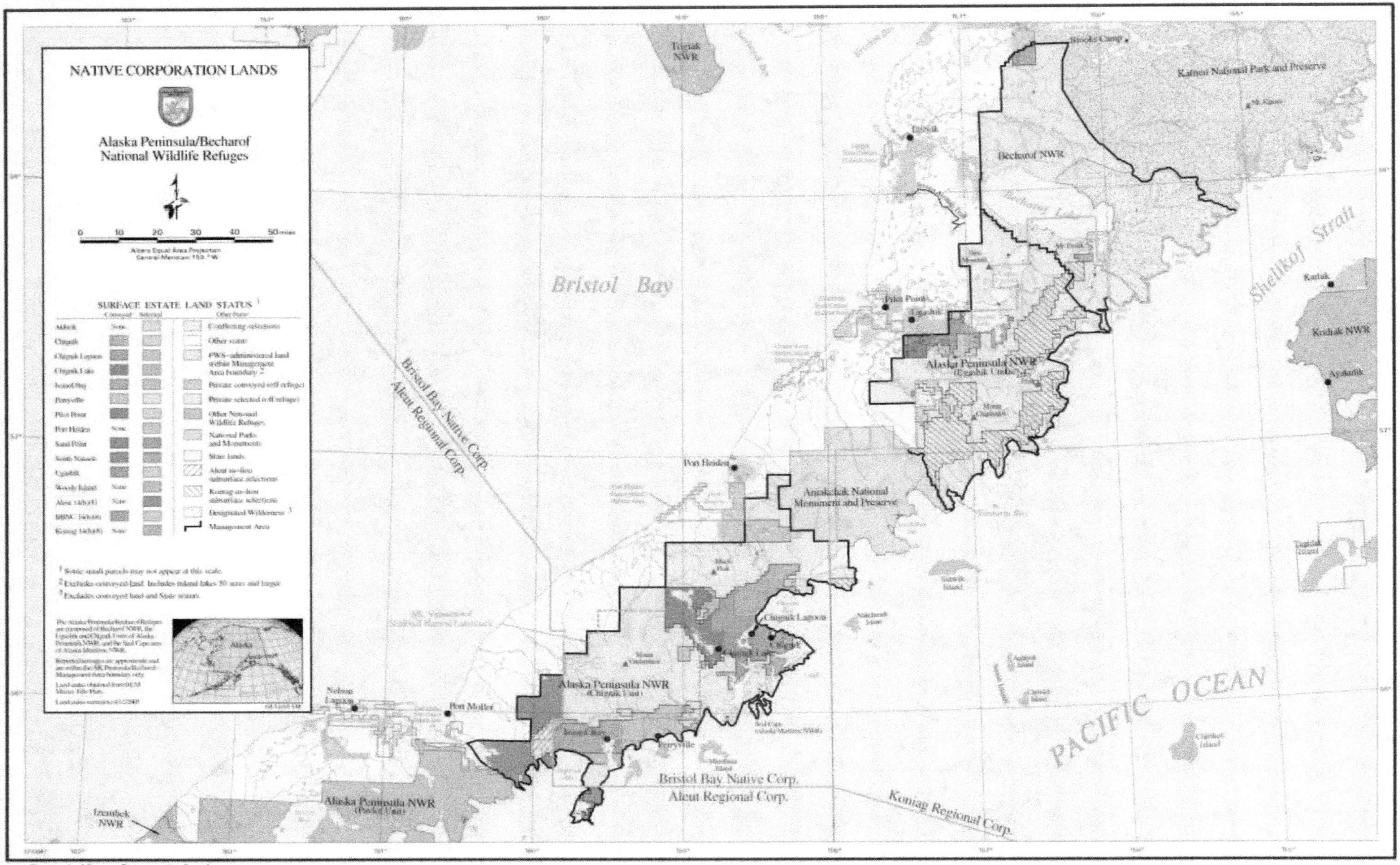

Alaska Peninsula and Becharof National Wildlife Refuges

Figure 8 Native Corporation Lands
Comprehensive Conservation Plan
131

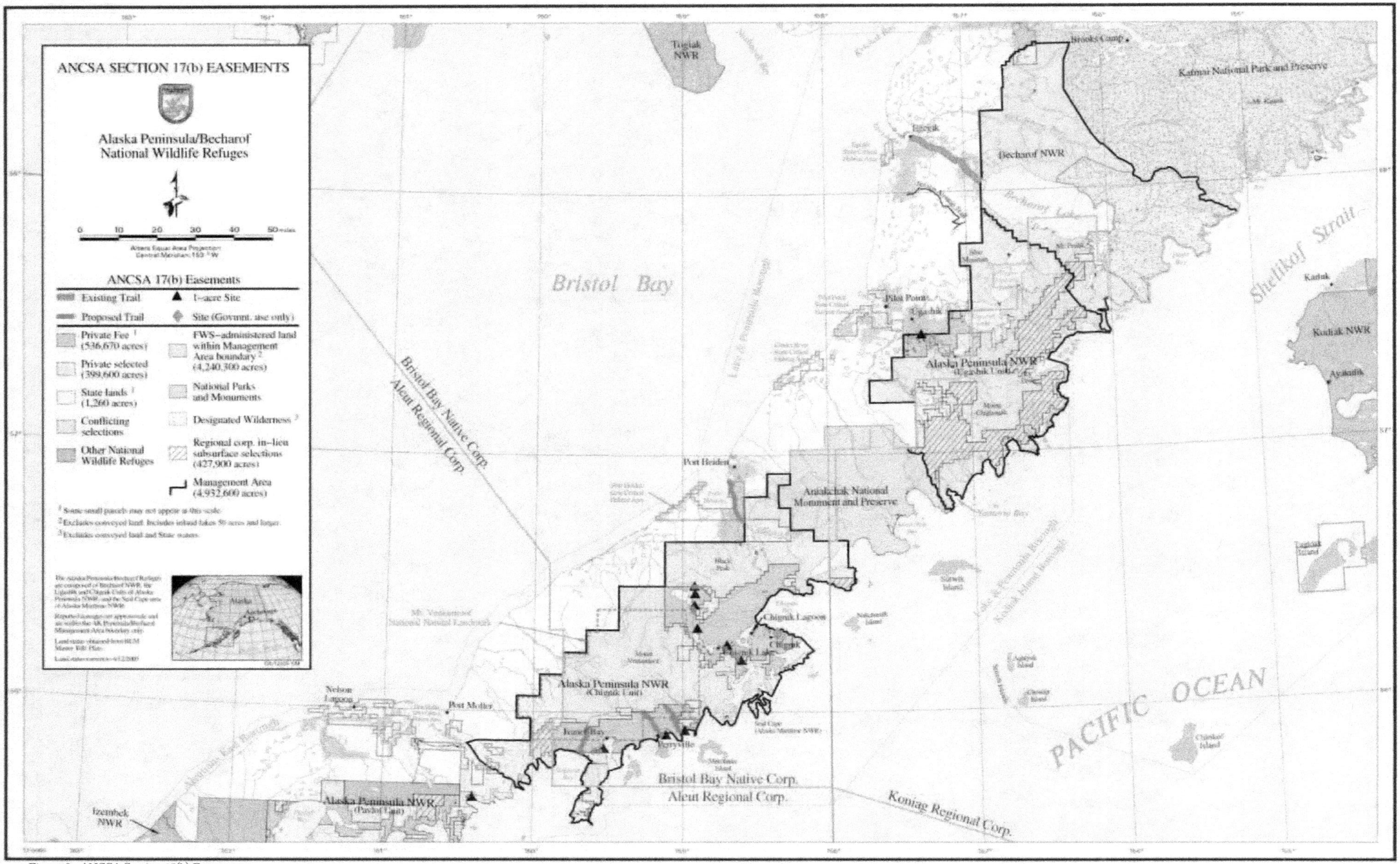

Figure 9   ANCSA Section 17(b) Easements
Comprehensive Conservation Plan
133

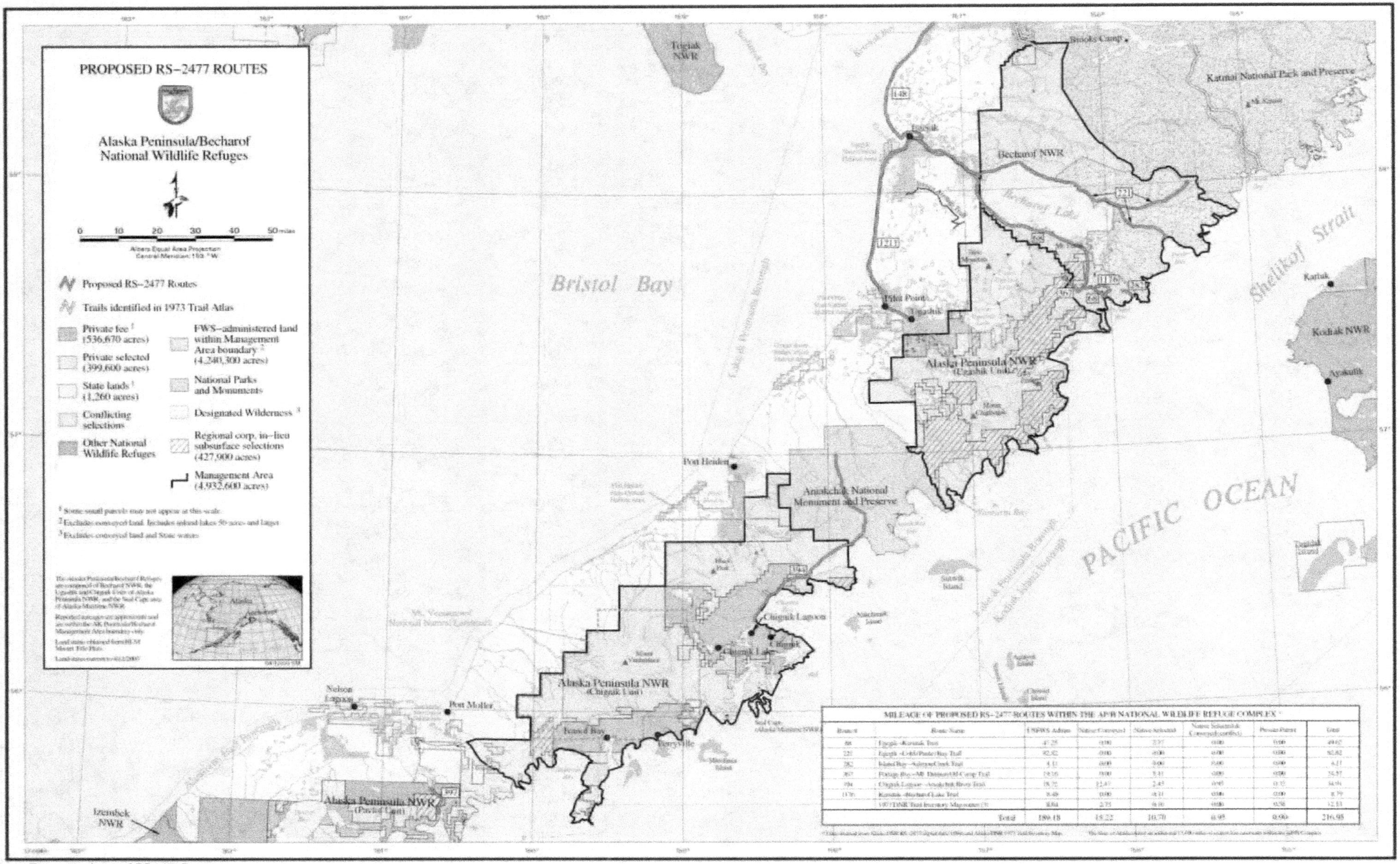

Figure 10   Asserted RS-2477 Routes
Comprehensive Conservation Plan
135